ut oo
print

89

The National Trust Book of
BRIDGES

Magdalen Bridge, Oxford. Over the Cherwell. 1772. By John Gwynn. With Magdalen College bell tower. See p.50.

The National Trust Book of
BRIDGES

J.M. Richards

JONATHAN CAPE
THIRTY BEDFORD SQUARE LONDON

First published 1984
Copyright © 1984 by J.M. Richards

Jonathan Cape Ltd, 30 Bedford Square, London WC1

British Library Cataloguing in Publication Data

Richards, J.M.
The National Trust book of bridges.
1. Bridges—Great Britain—History
I. Title
624′.2′0941   TG57

ISBN 0–224–02106–0

Printed in Great Britain by
Butler & Tanner Ltd
Frome and London

Contents

Introduction

There is no need to introduce this book with a disquisition on the fascination of bridges. They provide incidental pleasures to everyone travelling about the countryside, for in Britain their range and variety are remarkable. They illuminate our social history and the history of transport as well as being objects of interest in their own right. Regarded as works of architecture bridges possess the attraction that they can be appreciated without knowledge or understanding of what occurs out of sight, for the logic of their design is self-evident. A sound architectural precept is said to be that form follows function. In the case of a bridge the form *is* the function.

The visual satisfactions to be derived from bridges are enjoyably uncomplicated: the steady rhythm of arches receding in perspective; the texture of mellowed brick and stone in the ancient bridges of which a remarkable number survive throughout England, Wales and Scotland; the duplication of the shapes of arches as they are reflected in water, the latter rippling in the calmest weather as the bridges' cutwaters divide the flow of the stream.

This is to say nothing of the evidence, discernible in many old bridges, of other human uses than crossing from one side of a stream or river to the other. Thomas Hardy showed his appreciation of these when he wrote, in *The Mayor of Casterbridge*, of the two bridges – one brick, one stone – on the outskirts of the town of that name:

Every projection in each was worn down to obtuseness, partly by weather, more by friction from generations of loungers, whose toes and heels had from year to year made restless movements against these parapets, as they had stood there meditating on the aspect of affairs. In the case of the more friable bricks and stones even the flat faces were worn into hollows by the same mixed mechanism. The masonry at the top was clamped with iron at each joint; since it had been no uncommon thing for desperate men to wrench the coping off and throw it down the river, in reckless defiance of the magistrates. For to this pair of bridges gravitated all the failures of the town; those who had failed in business, in love, in sobriety, in crime. Why the unhappy hereabout usually chose the bridges for their meditations in preference to a railing, a gate, or a stile, was not so clear.

However such attributes of bridges as their appeal as places for lounging or meditating – unhappily or otherwise – are far outside the purpose of this book and relate in any case to only a few out of the many categories of bridge with which it must concern itself. More relevant are the beautiful landscape settings which bridges of almost every kind both enjoy and enhance, and the circumstance that the most agreeable views of a great number of towns and villages are obtained from the bridges over which they are approached. Hexham and Warkworth in Northumberland, Totnes in Devon and Aylesford in Kent are excellent examples. The many satisfactions offered by bridges of a later age include the spare elegance of suspension bridges and the noble rhythms of the great railway viaducts striding across valleys.

Unlike other historic monuments, old bridges are generally well looked after because to do so is a necessary concomitant of the upkeep of roads. This does not of course guarantee that any strengthening or widening that the growth of traffic may require is always tactfully done, but as it happens there are surprisingly few instances of clumsy adaptation to complain about. Even the bridges on private estates and in the parks of country houses, many of which are by distinguished architects – see Chapter 3 – have for the most part been well cared for in spite of rising costs, with just a few exceptions such as the elegant Basin Bridge by Sir William Chambers in the grounds of Woburn Abbey which is sadly neglected and defaced.

The account of the history and architecture of Britain's bridges that this book sets out to provide is arranged chronologically in the sense that it begins with the earliest surviving bridges, those of the Middle Ages, and follows the history up to the present day. But in the chapters devoted to bridges of specific types – such as early iron bridges, suspension bridges and footbridges – it has been thought least confusing to group all bridges of these types together, whatever their period; so the newest suspension bridges over the Severn, Forth and Humber will be found in the same chapter as the Menai suspension bridge of 1818. Because they hardly require a chapter to themselves, primitive types such as clapper bridges are included in the opening chapter on the Middle Ages although this type must have existed even earlier and, since the loosely piled stones of which they are composed may often have been replaced, their substance may well be later.

Since this book is not meant for specialists in bridge construction, technical terms have been avoided where possible* and descriptive words have sometimes

*There is a glossary at the end of the book defining the technical terms it has been necessary to use.

been used in a more general sense than specialists would approve of. For example the term 'cutwater' has been employed for all the projections formed to protect or strengthen the lower part of the piers of a bridge, whereas strictly a cutwater, as the word suggests, is a projection shaped specifically to divide the flow of the stream. A projection of a different shape should be termed a 'starling', but to do so would create more confusion since a starling may also consist of baulks of timber placed round the pier or cutwater to prevent damage from boats, floating tree-trunks or other debris and not part of the structure of the bridge.

The dates of bridges given in the following pages are the dates when they were designed or when construction was started. When the architects or engineers who designed bridges are known their names are of course given; also their dates when ascertainable (except in the cases of large engineering firms with many partners, and offices like those of county surveyors, where the partners or heads may very likely not have been the actual designers of the bridges for which they were nominally responsible). Dates of birth and death are given only when the architect or engineer is first mentioned, whether in the main text or in the annotated list of bridges at the end of each chapter.

These lists are selective only, a qualification that must be emphasized since they are not – could not possibly be – complete. They comprise the author's personal choice of bridges that in his view are especially worth looking at, that have some quality or unusual feature which makes them stand out from the others or that particularly well illustrate some point in the text. Readers may therefore find some of their favourite bridges absent; on the other hand it is hoped that their attention may be drawn to interesting specimens of which they were unaware. In these lists – although not in the main text – only bridges still in existence are included. In choosing which to include an attempt has been made to represent, in each category, as many regions of England, Wales and Scotland as possible.

The lists are arranged according to counties, and here some difficulties arise. A number of important bridges cross rivers which form the boundaries between counties. Which county are they in? The reader may have to look under both counties to find them. A more confusing difficulty is created by the (in the author's view deplorable) rearrangement of counties and changes in their names that resulted from the reform of the structure of Local Government that was announced in a White Paper in 1971 and implemented in 1974, a rearrangement particularly confusing for anyone who learnt his geography before 1974 and has not yet perhaps become accustomed to counties with names such as Avon, Humberside, Powys, Gwent and Grampian. The important bridge at Huntingdon, moreover, will be found under Cambridgeshire since Huntingdonshire no longer exists, and bridges in what used to be Worcestershire must be looked for under Hereford and Worcester.

To make matters more confusing, in Nikolaus Pevsner's invaluable county guides, *The Buildings of England*, which fortunately class bridges as buildings and to which the following pages owe much, the counties are the pre-1974 ones, and so some bridges now in Cambridgeshire – to mention only the one instance referred to above – will be found in the Pevsner volume on Huntingdonshire (in fact sharing one volume with Bedfordshire and Peterborough). Changes in boundaries moreover have shifted some important bridges from one county to another. Abingdon Bridge is in Pevsner's Berkshire volume; now it is in Oxfordshire.

In order to avoid confusion a single authority must be followed. The lists of selected bridges in this book are arranged (except for London being distinguished from Greater London) according to the county to which they are allocated in the gazetteer at the end of the Automobile Association's *Great Britain Road Atlas* – as likely as any other gazetteer to be consulted by readers travelling about Britain with an eye open for bridges.

October 1983   J.M.R.

1

The Middle Ages

Before the days of canal and railway transport the purpose of nearly all bridges was to cross rivers. Most replaced or supplemented a ford or a ferry, and the location and prosperity of towns, as well as the road system itself, was often determined by the siting of a bridge. Leland, the sixteenth-century antiquary and traveller, writes of the old St Nicholas Bridge at Salisbury, which in 1230 superseded the ford over the River Avon and survives to this day, that the result of building it was to divert the road westwards away from Wilton 'to the ruine of that towne'. Nor did Wilton ever return to being an important town in spite of the fame of its carpet industry. Leland similarly writes of Abingdon Bridge, first built over the Thames in 1416: 'the makynge of this bridge was a great hinderaunce to the towne of Walyngforde, whithar the trade was of them that came out of Glocestar-shire; but now they pass by Abingdon.'

The first bridges across British rivers, apart from short-lived expedients like tree-trunks thrown from bank to bank over a stream, were almost certainly those built by the Romans. No complete Roman bridges remain, but their stones survive in several places, for example near Corbridge, Northumberland, and a little further north at Chollerford on Hadrian's Wall can be seen the substantial bases of the stone piers and abutments of a Roman bridge over the upper reaches of the River Tyne, all in carefully dressed masonry. The remains of a wooden Roman bridge have been found near Chepstow. The locations of many Roman bridges – and of the stone causeways, pierced by culverts, that the Romans often built as an alternative to a bridge – are known for the reason just mentioned: towns grew up and flourished where they had made a river crossing practicable. The bridge over the Derwent at Stamford Bridge, Humberside, built as comparatively recently as 1723, is only a hundred yards or so east of the site of the Roman bridge which survived to become in 1066 the scene of the great battle named after it, in which Harald Hadrada, King of Norway, failed to prevent the advance of the English army northwards. 'And Harold King of the English', says the *Anglo-Saxon Chronicle*, 'then came over the bridge followed by his army, and there they made a great slaughter both of the Norwegians and of the Flemings.'

After the Romans left in A.D. 410 some knowledge of building skills was preserved by the religious orders, and since one of their concerns was to give aid to travellers, it was through their initiative that many of the first medieval bridges were built – see under Stoneleigh, Warwickshire, Tilford, Surrey, and Pershore, Hereford and Worcester, in the annotated list of bridges at the end of this chapter. In 1228 Walter Gray, Archbishop of York, granted an Indulgence to anyone contributing to 'the building of the bridge at Ottele' (Otley, West Yorkshire). The Cistercians, whose abbeys and monasteries were, by the rules of the order, remotely situated and who owned large tracts of agricultural land, and for both these reasons had need of good cross-country communications, were especially active as bridge builders.

The oldest medieval bridges now surviving are small in span because of their builders' limited technical ability, and in width because they were designed only for foot-passengers, horse-riders and pack-animals. There are good examples still in use at Charwelton, Northamptonshire, where the width between parapets is only three feet, at Sutton, Bedfordshire, and at West Rasen, Lincolnshire. There are many others that were subsequently widened to take wagons and other wheeled vehicles. At Barnstaple, Devon, the thirteenth-century bridge over the Taw has been widened several times and is now 24 feet wide including footways on both sides, but by looking under the arches it is still possible to see the 10-foot-wide structure of the original medieval bridge.

As well as being widened, Britain's large number of medieval bridges have naturally, over the years, needed repairing in various ways. The repair and maintenance of bridges was indeed a problem from the beginning. The king regularly issued 'grants of pontage' (licences to collect tolls for a limited period) to those charged with the maintenance of bridges, but there were continual complaints that the local magistracy neglected its duty to build and look after bridges. At Egginton, Derbyshire, it is recorded that in 1549 two bells from the parish church were sold in aid of 'repayrynge of the Muncks Brydge, wch is so farre in decay that the township is not able to amend the same'. Bridges are mentioned even in Magna Carta (signed in 1215); there was a clause which said that 'no village or individual shall be compelled to make bridges at river banks except those who from old were legally bound to do so'.

Many medieval bridges were of wood and have not survived, but a few still exist of the most primitive type of stone construction: flat slabs laid across piles of stones in the river bed. Just one stage removed from the even more primitive line of stepping-stones, they are known as clapper bridges. There are two famous examples in the West Country: At Postbridge on Dartmoor near the Moretonhampstead–Princetown road, which has three spans providing a level footway 6 ft 6 ins wide, and a longer one at Tarr Steps just in Somerset, resting on sixteen loose piles of stones. Both – though it cannot be proved – are claimed to be of Bronze Age date. Whether this is so or not, it is likely that individual stones will have been renewed from time to time. At the other end of England there is a clapper bridge at Linton in Wharfedale.

From the early Middle Ages the usual form of bridge construction was an arch or series of arches, with the intermediate piers resting on timber piles driven into the river bed. The earliest arch bridges were of stone; later, where stone was not available, they were of brick, for bricks were reintroduced from the Low Countries in the early thirteenth century. They had been freely used by the Romans, but after the Romans left Britain their manufacture was forgotten for nine hundred years. Arches, whether stone or brick, were constructed with the help of wooden centering such as is used for similar purposes today.

The shapes of the arches followed, in a general way, those current in Gothic building. Pointed arches were not often used in bridges after the fifteenth century; from then until the second half of the seventeenth century the four-centred Tudor arch was common and after that the round arch. Segmental arches however were used at all times from the early Middle Ages onwards.

To cross a narrow stream one arch was enough. A wider river required a series of arches, which was preferable to a single wide-span arch not only because the latter might have been beyond the builders' capacity to construct safely (though the great churches of the Middle Ages demonstrate what technical skill some masons of the time possessed) but because a series of small arches allowed the roadway they carried to remain comparatively level, whereas one great arch necessitated a steep rise and descent. Examples exist nevertheless of hump-backed single-arched bridges that date from the Middle Ages, such as the Brig O'Doon, Strathclyde (fifteenth century), and there are even some hump-backed bridges as recent as the eighteenth century – for instance at Pontypridd, Glamorgan, over the River Taff (1750). At Lanercost, Cumbria, there is a two-arched road bridge of 1724 which is exceptionally humped, creating very steep gradients. Even more exceptional – indeed unique in Europe – is the triangular bridge at Crowland, Lincolnshire, built in 1360 and composed of three arches meeting at the centre. It too has a very steep gradient, partly now of steps, and took foot-passengers and pack-animals over the Welland river which has since dried up.

A number of multi-arched medieval bridges have had a wider-span arch inserted later to facilitate navigation. Abingdon Bridge over the Thames, already mentioned, is an example. Navigation was not however the only reason why bridges were built with high-crowned arches, because the more usual low multi-arched bridges created something of a barrier to the flow of water down the river and were often – still sometimes are – swept away in times of flood.

When Celia Fiennes was travelling through the West Country in 1698 she rode into bad weather between Taunton and Okehampton. 'These rains', she wrote in her journal, 'fully convinced me of the need of so many great stone bridges whose arches were soe high, that I have wonder'd at it because the waters seemed shallow streames but they were so swelled by one night and dayes raine that they came up pretty near the arches, and ran in most places with such rapidity, and look'd so thick and troubled, as if they would clear all before them.'

To divert the rush of water beneath the arches, and to prevent damage by floating debris such as tree-trunks brought down by floods, as well as by carelessly steered boats, the piers supporting the arches were frequently re-inforced by cutwaters – triangular projections carried well above water level. Projections not designed to divide the flow of the stream should strictly be termed starlings rather than cutwaters, but see the disclaimer about technical terms in the Introduction to this book. Cutwaters are sometimes built on the upstream side of a bridge only, as for example at Thornborough, Buckinghamshire, and Pershore, Hereford and Worcester, and a further logical refinement, to be seen for example at Eashing, Surrey, is to make the cutwaters triangular on the upstream side of the bridge and rounded on the downstream side. In bridges with narrow roadways, the cutwaters or similar projections were often carried up to parapet level to house refuges for pedestrians. Good examples of old bridges where the cutwaters are extended upwards to fulfil this dual function are at Kingston Bagpuize, Oxfordshire (said to be the oldest bridge over the Thames – it was built in 1250), the fifteenth-century Crawford Bridge over the Stour at Spetisbury, Dorset, Old Stare Bridge at Stoneleigh over the Avon in Warwickshire and the bridge over the Dee at Llangollen, Clwyd.

Multi-arched bridges composed of a large number of low arches – often more like a causeway than a bridge – could create so great a barrier to the flow of water as to turn the space beneath the arches into a cataract and sometimes change the very nature of the river. An historic instance of this was the most famous of all medieval bridges, Old London Bridge. First constructed in 1176 (and until 1739, when the first Westminster Bridge was built, the only bridge across the Thames in the London area), it replaced a Roman bridge which, according to Dion Cassius, writing about A.D. 210, was in existence in A.D. 43, and then a sequence of Anglo-Saxon bridges of uncertain date. It consisted of twenty stone arches of varying width – none wide enough to allow the passage of anything but a smallish skiff or barge, although the seventh arch was replaced by a drawbridge to enable somewhat larger vessels to pass through – with the piers supporting the arches resting on wooden piles. Along its whole length was a street of timber-framed houses, more salubrious to live in than the nearby crowded city streets because of the fresh air blowing up the river.

The Great Stone Gate stood at its southern end and near the centre stood a splendid mansion, Nonesuch House. Among the dramatic results of bridging the river with such a structure was that upstream of it the water remained so placid and slow-moving that it froze over in severe winters, and downstream the force of the torrent pouring through the narrow arches scoured out the bed of the river to form a deep pool capable of taking the largest ships, to the lasting benefit of the port. Although the bridge was replaced centuries ago, this stretch of the river is still known as the Pool of London.

As well as facilitating passage over a river, some bridges were also equipped with the means of preventing it, especially at the approaches to towns. There fortifications of various kinds served the same purpose as the gateways at the approaches to castles – which also had, more often than not, drawbridges over a moat, a type of bridge outside the scope of this book. Mention has already been made of the gate that stood at one end of Old London Bridge, now no longer existing, but the Monnow Bridge, leading across the river of that name into the town of Monmouth, still has at the town end a fortified gate-tower, erected in 1296 and serving the additional purpose of halting traders for the payment of dues. The thirteenth-century Old Elvet Bridge over the Wear at Durham also had a fortified tower at one end, but this was demolished in 1760 at the same time as the city walls.

A very different kind of superstructure adorned a number of medieval bridges. This was a chapel, built as a shrine for the use of pilgrims and other travellers (and known as a chantry chapel) and also to collect donations for the upkeep of the bridge. Three medieval chantry chapels survive on English bridges: at St Ives, Cambridgeshire, at Rotherham, South Yorkshire, and at Wakefield, West Yorkshire. At Bradford-on-Avon, Wiltshire, a medieval bridge chapel was replaced in the seventeenth century by a domed lock-up which still stands. Old Elvet Bridge at Durham, as well as the tower just referred to, had two chapels, but these were demolished in the eighteenth century.

Throughout the Middle Ages the technique of bridge construction, whether stone or brick, varied very little, the most notable refinement being the introduction of ribbed arches to lighten the structure, to reduce the load on the foundations and during construction to eliminate some of the timber centering on which the arch-stones were laid. Two examples – out of a great many – of bridges with ribbed arches are those at East Farleigh, Kent (fifteenth century) and Eamont, Cumbria (1425), both of which have their ribbing elegantly echoed by recessed rings outlining each arch. The widest span of arch achieved in a British bridge in the Middle Ages, and surviving today, is that of the Twizel Bridge, Northumberland, which has a single stone arch with narrow chamfered ribs spanning 90 feet. Its date is unknown, but it was in existence in 1513 when it allowed the Earl of Surrey to cross the River Till not far from Berwick-on-

Tweed and compel the Scots to give battle at Flodden Field. Sir Walter Scott celebrates the event in *Marmion*:

> The Scots beheld the English host
> Leave Barmore wood, their evening post,
> And heedful watched them as they crossed
> The Till, by Twizel bridge.

Compared with most of England, Scotland (and Wales) possess fewer medieval bridges, being in those times relatively undeveloped and having much less road traffic. The same is true of the far south-west of England and of the mountainous north, both of which areas, like Scotland and Wales, were less populated and accessible and developed much more slowly. On the other hand such areas, notably Cornwall, have preserved a greater number of their medieval bridges unaltered. Some of these are unusually bold and impressive examples, no doubt because of the need to withstand the frequent raging torrents in winter and spring. The main improvement to Scotland's stock of bridges came later than the Middle Ages, in the mid-eighteenth century when General Wade, in the process of trying to open up the Highlands following the suppression of the Jacobite Rebellion with the help of a system of military roads, built a number of handsome bridges such as the 300-foot-long five-arched bridge over the Tay at Aberfeldy, Tayside. This has Classical embellishments, including obelisks on top of the abutments of the central arch, and brings us into the period when bridges were more consciously designed for architectural effect.

A Selection of Notable Medieval Bridges, listed by Counties (by Regions in Scotland)

England

Avon

Chew Magna   Tun Bridge over the Chew, a tributary of the Avon. Late fifteenth century. Stone. Three pointed arches, two with double arch-rings.

Limpley Stoke   Stokeford Bridge east of the village on the road to Winsley and Bradford-on-Avon. Exact date unknown (widened on the upstream side

1929). Replaced a ford over the Avon as its name implies. Bath stone. Four high segmental arches between prominent stepped cutwaters, the latter probably later than the arches.

Bedfordshire

Sutton (just north of Biggleswade)   Very early packhorse bridge, probably fourteenth century.

Buckinghamshire

Thornborough over the Tove   Fourteenth century. Stone. Six pointed arches with prominent arch-rings and cutwaters on the upstream side only.

Cambridgeshire

Huntingdon over the Ouse   1370. Stone. Six slightly pointed arches. Once bore a chapel.

St Ives over the Ouse   1414. Replaced an ancient wooden bridge. Barnack stone. Six ribbed arches of varying shape and span with cutwaters on both sides. Chantry chapel on south side of centre pier, consecrated 1426, now a museum.

St Ives, Cambs. Over the Ouse. 1414.

Wansford over the Nene where it forms the boundary with Northamptonshire. Thirteenth century but much restored, especially in 1577 (see tablet in parapet) after a storm in 1571, and in 1795 after two arches had been damaged by ice in the river. Stone. Ten round arches plus one wider elliptical arch (50-foot span) over the main stream. Round buttresses on piers of side arches. The bridge once carried the Great North Road but has now been bypassed.

Cheshire

Chester   Dee Bridge. 1407. Replaced a Norman bridge. Red sandstone. Seven arches of varying span, some pointed, some segmental; arch at southern end of later date. A tower, of which the base remains, once stood between the sixth and seventh arches. Widened 1825 (when a footwalk was corbelled out on the east side) by Thomas Harrison (1744-1829), the architect of the Grosvenor Bridge, Chester – see page 42.

Cornwall

Gunnislake   Linking Cornwall and Devon over the Tamar between Liskeard and Tavistock. 1520. Light-coloured granite. Six slightly pointed arches. Pedestrian refuges over triangular cutwaters.

Lawhitton   Greystone Bridge also linking Cornwall and Devon over the Tamar south-east of Launceston. 1439. Built by Bishop Lacey who granted an Indulgence to penitents contributing to the cost. Stone. Eight arches with cutwaters. An unusually fine specimen.

Lewannick   Trekelland Bridge over the Inney between Launceston and Liskeard. 1504. Granite. Three four-centred arches with cutwaters. Roadway only 10 feet wide; no footways.

Lostwithiel over the Fowey   1437 (parapets 1676). Stone. Five pointed arches of varying spans plus four added in the eighteenth century over a newly-cut channel. Typical low-arched Cornish bridge.

Stoke Climsland   The Horse Bridge over the Tamar. 1437. Local stone. Seven 20-foot spans with only a 12-foot roadway. Corbels projecting from the cutwaters on the upstream side believed to be meant for attaching fishing-nets. Another unusually fine specimen.

The Horse Bridge, Stoke Climsland, Cornwall. Over the Tamar. 1437.

Wadebridge over the Camel near its mouth   Leland wrote in 1538: 'Ther was a ferry 80 yeres syns and menne sumtyme passing over by horse stoode often in great jeopardie. The one Lovebone, Vicar of Wadebridge, movid with pitie began the bridge and with great paine and studie, good people putting their help thereto, finished it with XVII fair and great uniforme arches of stone.' It now has only fifteen arches and was widened in 1847 by building out segmental arches over the cutwaters, the medieval pointed arches being still visible beneath them. 400 feet long – the longest bridge in Cornwall.

Cumbria

Kirkby Lonsdale over the Lune (known as the Devil's Bridge)   Fifteenth century. Stone. Three high ribbed arches, the centre one – unusually – being the narrowest, outlined with double rings. Triangular cutwaters with polygonal balconies on top. No longer used for wheeled traffic. Jervoise the anthologist of bridges (see Bibliography) says that it is by far the finest bridge in the north of England.

Penrith   Eamont Bridge just south of the town, over the river of the same name. 1425, but succeeding an earlier bridge – grants of pontage recorded 1291. Widened 1832. Red sandstone. Three segmental arches outlined by strongly defined rings. Bold rounded cutwaters.

Eamont Bridge near Penrith, Cumbria. 1425.

Derbyshire

Bakewell over the Wye Fifteenth century (restored and widened nine-teenth century). Stone. Five pointed arches with ribs. Sharply triangular cutwaters housing pedestrian refuges.

Egginton (between Derby and Burton-on-Trent) over the Dove Monks Bridge. Early fifteenth century (one arch rebuilt 1695; widened 1703). Stone. Four segmental arches and bold cutwaters.

Devonshire

Barnstaple over the Taw Thirteenth century. Stone. Sixteen arches, thirteen early medieval; the other three, on the town side, replaced 1589. Widened 1834 (but medieval arches still visible beneath) when a footway was also added, carried on cast-iron brackets. A chapel once stood at the end of the bridge.

Bickleigh (five miles south of Tiverton) over the Exe Probably fourteenth century. Rubble stone. Five segmental arches. Low cutwaters.

Drewsteignton Fingle Bridge over the Teign, south-east of the village. Date unknown and may be post-medieval – perhaps seventeenth century. Granite. Three segmental arches separated by huge cutwaters.

Holne Bridge over the Dart on the eastern edge of Holne Moor Fifteenth

Postbridge, Devon. Clapper bridge over the East Dart.

century. Granite. Four semi-circular arches, two large and two small. Roadway only 10 feet wide; refuges in the parapets. A good specimen of an unaltered medieval bridge.

Postbridge over the East Dart on the eastern edge of Dartmoor Primitive clapper bridge. Local granite. Three 15-foot spans constructed of 6 ft 6 ins-wide slabs supported on piers, each of five flat stones. Steps at both ends. There are other, less well-preserved, clapper bridges on Dartmoor at Grimspound and Bellever Tor.

Fingle Bridge near Drewsteignton, Devon. Over the Teign. Probably late medieval.

Staverton over the Dart between Totnes and Ashburton   1413. One of the oldest unaltered arch bridges in the county. Stone. Seven obtusely pointed arches.

Dorset

Spetisbury   Crawford Bridge over the Stour, just east of the Blandford–Poole road. Fifteenth century. Replaced an earlier bridge built by the monks of Tarrant Abbey. Stone. Nine low segmental arches with cutwaters with pyramidal tops; the southern arches rebuilt 1819 (1719 date-stone not originally part of this bridge).

Sturminster Marshall   White Mill Bridge. Early fourteenth century (restored 1713). Stone. Eight arches with parapet walls corbelled out over the piers.

Sturminster Newton   Town Bridge over the Stour. Late medieval (widened seventeenth century). Stone. Six pointed arches.

County Durham

Barnard Castle over the Tees   1569 (repairs in 1596 indicated by inscribed stone in parapet; repaired again and parapets renewed after flood in 1771). Stone. Two pointed arches with triple rings.

Sturminster Newton, Dorset. Town Bridge over the Stour. Late medieval.

Old Elvet Bridge, Durham. Over the Wear. Begun 1160.

Durham   Old Elvet Bridge over the Wear, built by Bishop Pudsey 1160–1225 (repaired 1495; widened 1805). Two chapels added in the thirteenth century, one used later as a lock-up, and a row of houses and shops and a guard-tower which remained till 1760; in it James I was received during his progress to Scotland in 1617. Land arches still carry houses, one on the site of one of the chapels. Stone. Ten pointed arches with rings, only five spanning the river itself. The 1805 widening added semi-circular arches on the upstream side and four big cutwaters as buttresses.

Piercebridge carrying the Catterick road over the Tees where it forms the boundary with Yorkshire   Probably early sixteenth century (widened 1769). Stone. Three pointed arches with triple recessed rings.

Sunderland Bridge, four miles south of Durham   Over the Wear. About 1400. Stone. Four arches, one restored 1769; central arches with five ribs. Massive cutwaters.

Gloucestershire

Eastleach Martin over the Leach (which joins the Thames three miles below Lechlade) Clapper bridge. Date unknown (may be later than the Middle Ages). Three main spans resting on square stone piers.

Tewkesbury King John Bridge over the Avon (two bridges joined by a causeway). Originally built before 1205; frequently repaired and largely rebuilt in stone and concrete 1962 but with some old features remaining. One bridge has four arches, the other six; the causeway has seven land arches. Cast-iron cantilevered footways added to the bridge over the Old Avon.

Hampshire

Christchurch over the Avon Fifteenth century (widened 1900). Six stone arches – one blocked up – semi-circular with double rings.

Hereford and Worcester

Hereford Wye Bridge. 1490. Replaced an earlier bridge – grant of pontage recorded 1334 (widened 1826). Stone. Six arches with cutwaters, four original; four-centred and double-chamfered. One arch rebuilt segmental after the Civil War siege of 1645. At this time a gateway stood at

Wye Bridge, Hereford. 1490.

East Farleigh, Kent. Over the Medway. Fourteenth to fifteenth century.

the southern end. Greyfriars Bridge, a single-arch concrete bridge a little way upstream from the Wye Bridge, built in 1966, now takes most of the traffic.

Pershore   Old Bridge over the Avon. Originally 1290 (probably built by the monks of Pershore Abbey); repaired 1388 with material from abbey when this was demolished. Stone with brick parapets. Five round arches; centre arch larger. Latter demolished in 1644 by Royalist army to impede pursuit by Parliamentary troops under Waller and afterwards repaired. Cutwaters on upstream side only.

Wilton (south-west of Ross-on-Wye) over the Wye   1597 – rights of pontage granted 1599 to Charles Bridges in compensation for his loss of ferry-rights at the same spot. Red sandstone. Six semi-circular arches, one rebuilt after the Civil War. Unusually massive cutwaters with pedestrian refuges.

Kent

Aylesford over the Medway   Fourteenth century. Replaced a ford. Kentish ragstone. Built on a curve. Originally eight pointed arches; two centre ones replaced by a single segmental arch 1824.

East Farleigh over the Medway   Fourteenth or fifteenth century (repaired 1843). Kentish ragstone. Five pointed arches, four with narrow chamfered ribs. Bulky cutwaters on both sides, sloped at the top. Jervoise describes it as 'certainly the finest bridge in the South of England'.

15

Yalding   Three bridges: the Town Bridge over the Beult, Twyford Bridge over the Medway and Laddingford Bridge over the Teise. Exact dates unknown. Kentish ragstone. Twyford Bridge has four arches with large cutwaters incorporating pedestrian refuges; the other two have seven and two arches respectively.

Lancashire

Hornby   Loyn Bridge over the Lune. Sixteenth century. Stone. Three segmental arches with prominent cutwaters.

Paythorne over the Ribble   Date unknown. Stone. Two ribbed arches; massive pier with prominent cutwater between. Widened on the upstream side.

Leicestershire

Leicester   Aylestone Bridge over the Soar. Fifteenth-century packhorse bridge only 4 feet wide between parapets. Stone. Ten low arches, two relined later in brick. Cutwaters.

Lincolnshire

Crowland   Trinity Bridge over three streams (now dry) where the Nene, the Welland and the Catwater Drain meet. 1360. Ancaster limestone. Three ribbed arches, outlined by mouldings and meeting in the centre; one approached by steps. Originally crowned by a canopied cross. Now has a seated figure brought from Crowland Abbey in 1720.

Lincoln   High Bridge over the Witham. 1540. Stone (now reinforced with iron). One arch. One of the few surviving bridges in England with houses superimposed – of four storeys in this case, the upper two half-timbered. All now much restored.

West Rasen   Packhorse bridge over the Rase. Fourteenth century. Stone. Three ribbed arches. Only 4 ft 6 ins wide between parapets.

Norfolk

Buxton (between Aylsham and Coltishall)   Mayton Bridge over the Bure.

16

Crowland, Lincs. Triangular Trinity Bridge. 1360.

Fifteenth century. Stone. Two pointed arches. Niches providing covered seats at both ends.

Cringleford (south-west of Norwich) over the Yare   1520. Stone. Two four-centred arches. Widened 1780, partly in brick by adding new rings of arches on each side, springing from the original cutwaters, but with an elegantly coherent result. Survived the great flood of 1912 when eighty Norfolk bridges were swept away.

Twizel Bridge, Tweedmouth, Northumberland. Over the Till. Around 1500.

Norwich Bishops Bridge over the Wensum. 1249. Brick and stone, faced with flint. Three semi-circular arches. It once had a gateway, later occupied by a hermit; this was demolished in the nineteenth century.

Northamptonshire

Charwelton over the Cherwell Early medieval packhorse bridge, only 3 feet wide between parapets. Two pointed stone arches.

Irthlingborough over the Nene Fourteenth century. Stone, but one arch rebuilt in brick. Nineteen arches, nine forming the approaches. Widened in the nineteenth century on the upstream side.

Wakerley over the Welland Fourteenth century. Stone. Five pointed arches with double chamfered rings, cutwaters between. 81 feet long. 10-foot roadway widened in the eighteenth century to 12-foot by adding segmental arches on the upstream side.

18

Northumberland

Lesbury over the Aln (near its mouth) Date unknown but undoubtedly medieval. Stone. Two arches, one pointed, one segmental, both with double rings. Widened on downstream side; massive cutwaters on upstream side.

Tweedmouth Twizel Bridge near Berwick-on-Tweed over the Till. Around 1500. Stone. One high round arch of 90-foot span with five narrow chamfered ribs.

Warkworth over the Coquet north of Amble 1379. Red sandstone. Two segmental ribbed arches with a massive cutwater on the pier between. Tower at southern end. Now pedestrian only.

Oxfordshire

Abingdon over the Thames 1416. Replaced an ancient ferry. Built by the Fraternity of the Holy Cross (mostly composed of local wool-merchants). The Fraternity, being associated with the recently dissolved Abingdon Abbey, was suppressed in 1553 but maintenance of the bridge, along with that at Culham (see below) was made the responsibility of the local Christ's Hospital.

Warkworth Bridge, Northumberland. Over the Coquet. 1379.

Four pointed arches and a 20-foot-wide navigation arch inserted 1790; largely rebuilt 1927 but first two arches on town side original. A second part, of seven arches, crosses a millstream alongside.

Burford over the Windrush   Fourteenth century (a predecessor was reported as being in ruinous condition and pontage granted for its repair). Stone. Four very low segmental arches between wide and prominent cutwaters creating an unusual zig-zag form. Parapet rebuilt 1945.

Culham   Old Bridge over a backwater of the Thames, south of the newer bridge on the Dorchester road. 1416 (widened 1790). Built by the Abingdon Guild of the Holy Trinity. Stone. Five pointed arches of varying spans. No longer carries wheeled traffic.

Kingston Bagpuize over the Thames   1250 (claimed to be the oldest Thames bridge, but that at Radcot – see below – may be older). Six pointed arches, the middle one wider. They once all had stone ribs but some were removed in 1793 to improve clearance. Cutwaters housing pedestrian refuges.

Radcot over a backwater of the Thames between Bampton and Faringdon   Thirteenth or fourteenth century (in 1393 a grant was made for the repair of the bridge after damage during the wars between Richard II and the barons). Stone. Two outer arches pointed with four wide ribs; centre arch (presumably later) four-centred. Reputedly the oldest Thames bridge, but so is that at Kingston Bagpuize – see above.

Shropshire

Ludlow   Ludford Bridge over the Teme. Mid-fifteenth century. Replaced a Norman bridge. Stone. Three semi-circular arches, each of 30-foot span, between unusually bulky cutwaters. Once carried a chapel.

Somerset

Haselbury (near Crewkerne) over the Parrett   Fourteenth or fifteenth century. Stone – unusually substantial. Two pointed arches with prominent chamfered ribs.

Tarr Steps   Clapper bridge over the Barle, near the village of Hawkridge south of Exmoor. Date unknown. Seventeen spans consisting of loose piles of stones supporting stone slabs 5 feet wide. Partly demolished by a flood in 1952 but thoroughly restored.

Staffordshire

Sandon over the Trent   Fifteenth century. Stone. Two arches, one with five ribs, the other with four. Prominent cutwaters with pedestrian refuges.

Shugborough over the Trent (also known as Essex Bridge), passing through Shugborough Park about six miles east of Stafford   Sixteenth century. Stone. Fourteen segmental arches. Width between parapets only 4 feet but pedestrian refuges in cutwaters – see also Chapter 3.

Suffolk

Hadleigh   Toppesfield Bridge over the Brett on the road to Lower Layham. Fourteenth century. Stone with some brick facing and brick parapets. Three pointed arches with chamfered ribs.

Surrey

Tilford over the Wey, probably built by Cistercian monks from Waverley Abbey after a great flood in 1233 when many bridges in the area were swept away. There are two bridges in different parts of the village, one of seven and the other of five round arches. Rough Bargate stone. Cutwaters pointed on the upstream side and rounded on the downstream. There are similar rough stone thirteenth-century bridges, also over the Wey, at Eashing and Elstead not far away.

Sussex, West

Stopham over the Arun between Pulborough and Petworth   1423. Replaced a wooden bridge of 1347 which had itself replaced a ferry. Sussex sandstone. Six round arches of varying spans with a wider and higher segmental arch (1822) over the main channel. Pedestrian refuges in semi-hexagonal bays over the cutwaters.

Trotton over the Rother between Petersfield and Midhurst   Early fifteenth century. Stone. Five semi-circular arches with chamfered ribs.

Stopham, Sussex. Over the Arun. 1423.

Warwickshire

Stoneleigh   Old Stare Bridge over the Avon near the Coventry-Leamington road. Thirteenth century. Built by Cistercian monks from Stoneleigh Abbey. Sandstone. Three river arches plus six flood arches. Massive cutwaters forming piers as wide as the arches. A good example of an unaltered medieval bridge.

Stratford-upon-Avon   Clopton Bridge, on the site of the Saxon ford after which the town was named. 1480. Local stone. Built by Sir Hugh Clopton, a local merchant who was Lord Mayor of London in 1492. Repaired 1588 after flood damage and again in 1642 after one arch had been blown up to impede Cromwell's army. Widened 1811. Toll-house, in the form of a small ten-sided tower with battlemented roof-parapet, added at the town end in 1814. Iron footway added on upstream side 1827. Fourteen pointed arches.

Water Orton (near Birmingham) over the Tame   Sixteenth century. Built by the Bishop of Exeter. Six semi-circular arches. Bold triangular cutwaters with refuges.

22

Tilford, Surrey. Over the Wey. Thirteenth century. See p. 21.

Clapham, North Yorks. Medieval packhorse bridge over the Clapham Beck. See p. 24.

The medieval Usk Bridge, Crickhowell, Powys. See p. 28.

Brig O'Doon, near Ayr, Strathclyde. Fifteenth century. See p. 29.

Bradford-on-Avon, Wilts. Fourteenth century.

Wiltshire

Bradford-on-Avon   Fourteenth century. Nine stone arches (one buried under
northern approach), two original, pointed with chamfered ribs; remainder
round, rebuilt in seventeenth century. Medieval chantry chapel between, rebuilt after the Reformation as a lock-up with domed roof surmounted by a
wind-vane; later used as a powder-magazine.

Clopton Bridge, Stratford-upon-Avon, Warwicks. 1480.

Salisbury St Nicholas Bridge, Harnham (over the Avon just south of the cathedral). Built 1230 by Bishop Bingham over two streams of the river. Stone. The shorter section has two arches (plus one filled in) with cutwaters; the longer section six pointed arches. Widened on both sides 1774. A chapel once stood on the island between the two streams.

Yorkshire, North

Clapham Narrow packhorse bridge in centre of village over Clapham Beck. Date unknown. Stone. Single arch, with picturesquely undulating rounded parapet.

Croft over the Tees south of Darlington, where it forms the Yorkshire–County Durham boundary Fifteenth century (widened 1795). Stone. Seven pointed arches with narrow ribs.

Haxby Packhorse bridge over the Nidd, about three miles north of York. Date unknown (may be later than the Middle Ages). Stone. Single arch of 64-foot span, slightly hump-backed.

Knaresborough High Bridge over the Nidd. Exact date unknown. Stone. Widened 1826 but two medieval arches with chamfered ribs visible beneath.

Wensley over the Ure on the road to West Witton Fourteenth century. Stone. Three arches, two pointed and one (later) segmental. Cutwaters with sloping tops.

St Nicholas Bridge, Harnham, Salisbury, Wilts. Over the Avon. 1230.

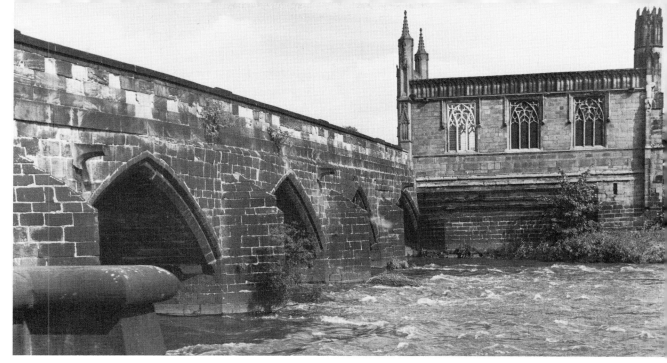

Wakefield, West Yorks. Over the Calder. 1350.

Yorkshire, South

Rotherham over the Don on the site of an ancient ford   1483 (widened in the eighteenth century but reduced again to original width after construction of a new bridge upstream in 1928). River now flows, except in times of flood, under only one arch. Stone. Four pointed arches ribbed underneath. Chantry chapel (also 1483) founded by Archbishop of York. After dissolution of chantries in 1547 it became an almshouse, then a gaol (until 1826), then a tobacconist's shop. Restored as a chapel in 1924.

Yorkshire, West

Otley over the Wharfe   Exact date unknown; probably thirteenth century. Stone – very robust. Seven arches, five ribbed; other two (rebuilt after a flood in 1673) not.

Wakefield over the Calder   1350 (since widened). Stone. Nine pointed arches (round on west side where widened). Superseded for wheeled traffic by new bridge 1933. Chantry chapel near east end endowed by Edward III in 1358 (only bridge chapel in England besides Rotherham – see above – still used for services). Rich Decorated style. Restored 1847 by Sir George Gilbert Scott (1811–78); again in 1939 by Sir Charles Nicholson (1867–1949).

25

WALES

Clwyd

Holt over the Dee where it forms the boundary with Cheshire 1545. Red sandstone. Eight segmental arches separated by bold cutwaters. Originally incorporated a drawbridge with guard-tower and gateway of which traces remained until late nineteenth century.

Llangollen over the Dee 1131. Rebuilt 1346 by the Bishop of St Asaph and again around 1500; widened on upstream side 1873. Stone. Four pointed arches with prominent cutwaters containing pedestrian refuges.

Dyfed

Devil's Bridge over the deep ravine of the Mynach Three superimposed bridges, only the lowest medieval. Twelfth century; believed to have been built either by the monks of Strata Florida Abbey or by the Knights Hospitaller who owned land near by. One pointed stone arch. The middle arch, also stone, was built in 1753 and the upper, which now carries the roadway and consists of a lattice steel girder between stone abutments, in 1900.

Glamorgan

Bridgend New Inn Bridge over the Ogmore, about a mile below the town. Fourteenth century. Limestone. Four pointed arches of varying spans.

Gwent

Monmouth Monnow Bridge over the Monnow. 1272. Stone. Three arches. Fortified gate-tower at town end built 1296 for the collection of dues; licence to collect these granted by Edward I to raise money for building walls to protect upper part of the town. During the Civil War both sides in turn occupied the tower. In 1839 it was garrisoned by soldiers when the Chartists were thought to be about to attack Monmouth gaol. It no longer has its portcullis and doors. The bridge was originally no wider than the tower archway; the later widening has however left the ribs of the medieval arches still visible.

Gwynedd

Dinas-Mawddwg Gwanas Old Bridge over the Dyfi between Dolgellau and Welshpool (road now diverted). Packhorse bridge. Exact date unknown. Stone. Two 19-foot segmental arches.

Powys

Brecon Usk Bridge. 1563. Stone. Replaced a bridge destroyed by floods in 1535. Widened 1794 by Thomas Edwards (who was possibly one of the sons of the celebrated Welsh bridge-builder – see next chapter) and again in 1801 by Arthur Maund (1722–1803). Seven arches of varying spans.

Monnow Bridge, Monmouth, Gwent. 1272.

Crickhowell over the Usk Date uncertain; widened. Stone. Twelve arches. 406 feet long.

SCOTLAND

Central

Stirling Auld Brig over the Forth, known in history as 'the key to the Highlands'. Around 1400 but replacing a still earlier bridge. Sandstone. Four round arches; the piers between resting on enlarged starlings like islands. No longer used for wheeled traffic since the Stirling–Perth road was diverted in 1831 over a new bridge (see next chapter) designed by the Scottish engineer Robert Stevenson.

Dumfries and Galloway

Dumfries Old Bridge over the Nith. 1432 (partly rebuilt 1620). Stone. Originally nine round arches; now six. No longer carries wheeled traffic because in 1794, when a new five-arch bridge was built by Thomas Boyd (1753–1822), the three spans on the town side were demolished and replaced by eleven steps.

Fife

Leuchars Guard Bridge over the Eden estuary south of Cupar. 1450. Stone. Six arches of varying spans.

Grampian

Aberdeen Bridge of Dee. 1527 (repaired 1718 and 1722; widened 1841 by the Aberdeen architect John Smith, 1781–1852). Elgin sandstone and granite. Seven almost semi-circular arches ribbed underneath. Inscriptions and coats of arms on south side.

Aberdeen Brig O'Balgownie over the Don. 1320 (reconstructed 1607). Sandstone and granite. Single pointed arch of 70-foot span. 35 feet high. Stepped parapets.

Brig O'Balgownie, near Aberdeen. Over the Don. 1320

Strathclyde

Ayr   The Auld Brig over the Ayr in the centre of the town. Late thirteenth century (repaired 1910). Sandstone. Four slightly pointed arches of 57-foot span between massive cutwaters with steeply sloping tops. For pedestrians only since the New Bridge, built a short way downstream in 1785, had to be replaced by yet another in 1877, thus to some extent fulfilling the prophecy in Robert Burns's poem – see page 30.

Bothwell Brig over the Clyde south-east of Glasgow   1400. Bothwell Park stone. Four round arches. Cantilevered iron footways added.

Brig O'Doon over the Doon two or three miles south of Ayr   Fifteenth century. Single stone arch of 70-foot span, steeply humped. Wheeled traffic now uses nearby bridge built 1832.

29

2

The Improved Highway: Seventeenth to Nineteenth Centuries

Just as house builders, especially in remote parts of Britain, continued long after the Middle Ages to build in the manner they had inherited from their fathers, so was bridge-building also slow to adopt the changes in architectural style, influenced by the Italian Renaissance, that had been taken up in the cities and among the more fashion-conscious builders of country mansions from the sixteenth century onwards. This conservatism is exemplified by the bridge over the Thames at Sonning, Berkshire – more precisely over the main channel of the divided river. Though not built until late in the eighteenth century, Sonning Bridge is hardly different, with its eleven low brick arches of varying spans and its steepish gradient and narrow carriageway, from the medieval bridges described in the last chapter. The role of a river bridge had not changed and the new styles of architecture, here and elsewhere, had hardly begun to make themselves felt.

Nevertheless a certain amount of scorn was beginning to be expressed about Britain's crumbling medieval bridges and their dilatory and insufficient replacement. At the same time the growth of antiquarianism, fostered in eighteenth-century literature, led to an opposite view. The conflict between the two views is reflected in Robert Burns's long poem 'The Brigs of Ayr', written in 1786. Its form is a dialogue between the old and the new bridges over the River Ayr in the centre of the Scottish town of that name. In the course of the dialogue the New Brig asks:

> Will your poor narrow foot-path of a street,
> Where twa wheel-barrows tremble when they meet,
> Your ruin'd formless hulk o' stone and lime,
> Compare wi' bonnie brigs o' modern time?

To which the Auld Brig answers:

Sonning Bridge, Berks. Over the Thames. 1773.

This mony a year I've stood the flood an' tide;
And tho' wi' crazy eild I'm sair forfairn,
I'll be a brig, when ye're a shapeless cairn.

The eighteenth century had seen very little effort made to maintain old bridges. The local justices were responsible for maintenance and repair, their frequent dilatoriness being illustrated by the experience of Lanercost, Cumbria (see page 43). However as the century progressed new and more up-to-date bridges were constructed in some numbers in response to the growth of traffic. In these a more consciously sophisticated architectural expertise gradually took over; witness Maidenhead Bridge only a short way down the Thames from Sonning, built in 1772 to a design by Sir Robert Taylor (1714–88) with its chamfered voussoirs outlining each arch, its dentilled string-course and its elegant balustrade – a far cry from the naivety of Sonning Bridge though almost exactly contemporary with it. To treat a bridge as a monument was an ambition of a new kind and an increasing number of well-known architects began turning their talents towards bridge design, often guided in matters like

Maidenhead Bridge, Berks. Over the Thames. 1772. By Sir Robert Taylor.

the construction of arches by the ever more versatile – and often amateur – men of science.

The architects of the many bridges built at this time relied on the same arch construction in stone or brick as the medieval masons who preceded them, though their arches were generally wider in span and either segmental or semi-circular in shape. In spite, however, of their relatively orthodox construction, the building of these multi-arch stone bridges was not always completed without problems, especially when they crossed wide rivers with powerful tides and currents. These problems, as well as the pride taken in new bridges as civic improvements – notably in London where a single medieval bridge had been made to suffice for centuries – are illustrated by the following passage describing the construction of the second bridge over the Thames, Westminster Bridge, in Daniel Defoe's *A Tour Thro' the Whole Island of Great Britain*, published in 1761.

The first Pile of this Bridge was driven in 1738 and the Whole was finished, and ready to be opened for Use, in Autumn 1747, when it was discovered that the 5th Pier from the *Westminster* Side was sinking; and soon after Stones fell out of the Arch next to it. It was necessary therefore to take off the Arches that rested on the Pier; which was done with great Care, by replacing Centres under them, like those on which they were turned. The sinking Pier was then loaded with 12.000 Ton of Cannon and Leaden Weights, in order to sink and settle it. This, and the Deliberations how to repair the Defect, took up above a Year: But in the Summer of 1749, Materials being ready, it was intirely finished for Use, and opened *Nov.* 17. 1750. at Midnight. The Pier that had failed, was freed from its Burden by a secret Arch now not to be seen.

If we consider its Length, its Breadth, the Regularity of the Design, the Beauty of the Workmanship, the great inland Navigation, which it does not impede, the Avenues that lead to it, the Provision made for the Defence of Passengers against the Weather in their Way over it, the Watch of 12 men every Night for the Security of their Persons, and the beautiful globular Lamps, 16 on each Side, suspended on Irons that project inwards, with a lofty Sweep, from the top of each Recess, and on the Sides of the Abutments, softening the Horrors of the Night, and diffusing a star-like Radiance, not only over the circumfluent Waters, but over the circumjacent Lands, and princely Palaces; all these Circumstances may well seem to give this Bridge a Superiority over most other Bridges mentioned in History.

The edifice so enthusiastically welcomed by Defoe was a fifteen-arched bridge designed by a Swiss architect, Charles Labelye (1705–81). It was the first bridge – perhaps the first masonry structure – to use solid piers of Portland stone instead of filling the interiors of the piers with rubble as was the traditional practice. Labelye's bridge was replaced by the present Westminster Bridge in 1854.

The eighteenth-century architects, when they came to design bridges, employed – simply or ornately – the Classical vocabulary that had by then been current for two hundred years. James Paine (1717–89) was a diligent bridge builder. He designed Richmond and Chertsey Bridges, also over the Thames, as well as several in the parks of the country houses of which he was the architect – see the next chapter; and there were architects who specialized in bridges, such as John Gwynn (1713–86) and Robert Mylne (1733–1811). The latter was a friend of James Boswell (who mentions Mylne in his *London Journal*) and first became known as a result of winning, in 1760, the competition for yet another bridge over the Thames in London: Blackfriars Bridge – a competition for which most of the leading architects of the day entered. Mylne's victory followed a prolonged controversy caused by his proposal to use elliptical arches, hitherto unknown in Britain for any but small-span bridges such as that at Aberffraw, Anglesey (see page 52). The idea was to provide wider openings than semi-circular arches would have done without increasing their height. Mylne's Blackfriars Bridge was completed in 1769 and replaced with the present one by Joseph Cubitt (1811–72), exactly a hundred years later.

Another architect who specialized in bridges was the Welshman William Edwards (1719–89) of Pontypridd. Edwards was self-taught, having started as a mason. He in fact designed little else but bridges, and he had three sons who also became bridge builders. Many other architects who by the end of the century had mastered – or at least learnt to employ – the new Classical vocabulary were called on to design the occasional bridge, and almost the contemporary of Mylne was John Smeaton (1724–92), one of the first of the great civil engineers – a term he invented. Although they appeared on opposing sides in several bridge-building controversies, including that over Blackfriars, Smeaton and Mylne maintained a respect for each other. Their rivalry however marks the significant moment when the architectural and engineering professions began to go their separate ways (most important bridges were designed by architects until about 1790; afterwards by engineers). Mylne had had the usual architectural training in Rome; Smeaton by contrast was self-taught. He never styled himself anything but an engineer and denied any competence in what he called 'the ornamental parts of architecture'.

Smeaton, whose major bridges are in Scotland at Coldstream, Borders (1763), Perth (1765) and Banff (1772), was followed by a remarkable sequence of civil engineers who dominated the constructional enterprises, and especially the bridges, associated with the Industrial Revolution – which indeed they helped to create. The greatest were Thomas Telford (1757–1834) and John Rennie (1761–1821) whose work we shall be examining in later chapters. They and their successors, the railway engineers, were responsible for revolutionary developments in bridge design, but these did not come until the very end of the eighteenth century and the beginning of the nineteenth. Throughout most of the eighteenth century the designs produced by the professional architects represented only the cosmetic aspects of change. The significant and lasting changes were functional ones arising from changes in the traffic using bridges and in the quality of road surfaces.

Long after the end of the Middle Ages road-travel even in the more civilized parts of Britain remained arduous and precarious. Heavy goods continued to be carried by water, down the navigable parts of rivers or from port to port in coastal vessels. Wheeled vehicles were relatively few; mostly wagons restricted to local use. Lighter loads were carried on strings of pack-animals. Packhorse bridges, a type only to be associated, it might be thought, with the elementary transport methods of the Middle Ages, were still enough for many localities' needs and were still being constructed. There is, for example, a surviving packhorse bridge (among many in the north) at Ovingham, Northumberland, that dates only from the end of the seventeenth century.

Coldstream Bridge, Borders. Over the Tweed. 1763. By John Smeaton.

Individual travellers went on horseback, but even for horses the roads were barely adequate, many being little more than tracks. The observant Celia Fiennes, quoted in the last chapter, made all her journeys on horseback, often in considerable discomfort because of the state of the roads. In 1698 she was travelling through Cornwall: ' ... and then', she wrote,

I came down a very steep stony hill to Louu, and here I cross'd a little arme of the sea on a bridge of 14 arches ... and soe I continued up and down hill. Here indeed I met with more inclosed ground and soe had more lanes and a deeper clay road, which by the raine the night before had made it very dirty and full of water; in places in the road there are many holes and sloughs where ever there is clay ground, and when by raines they are filled with water its difficult to shun danger; here my horse was quite down in one of these holes full of water.

Cornwall was of course still a backward area, but similar conditions were to be met with almost everywhere. What was worse was the disconcerting experience of seventeenth- and eighteenth-century travellers that in many parts of the country the roads, rather than improving since the Middle Ages, had deteriorated. They continued to do so as the number of wheeled vehicles increased, in spite of attempts in the middle of the seventeenth century to set legal limits to the size and weight of vehicles to minimize the damage caused – an interesting parallel to the concern expressed today over increasing lorry weights. In addition droves of cattle and herds of sheep on their way to market or being moved about the countryside caused damage to the soft road surfaces.

At the same time the bridges that had served the country throughout the Middle Ages were becoming insufficient for the increasing quantity and weight of wheeled traffic. When Defoe was travelling in Devonshire in 1725 he described the bridge at Bideford as so narrow that 'they are so chary of it that few carriages go over it; but as the water ebbs quite out of the river every low water, the carts and wagons go over the sands with great ease and safety'. Bideford Bridge was widened in 1815 and largely rebuilt in the 1860s.

The structure of many bridges moreover was deteriorating. The levying of tolls for the upkeep of bridges had lapsed and bridges dependent on the alms of passers-by were no longer being supported because after the Reformation there was no one to collect the alms. Some bridges fell into such a ruinous state that the fords they had superseded were brought into use again. Although the regular repair and improvement of old bridges, as well as the provision of more capacious ones, was better organized in the eighteenth century, it was not until the nineteenth that the maintenance of bridges was made the responsibility of the county authorities. Concern for the care of bridges as objects of antiquity took no official form until 1919 when the Ancient Monuments Board, following the passing of the Ministry of Transport Act which provided finance for the improvement of roads and bridges, asked the architect and antiquarian W. R. Lethaby (1857–1931) to compile a list of old bridges – eighteenth-century or earlier – deserving of careful treatment if they had to be repaired or widened. This action was followed by the compilation of the books by Edwyn Jervoise, sponsored by the Society for the Protection of Ancient Buildings, included in the Bibliography on page 203.

It was largely because of the poor state of roads and bridges even as late as the eighteenth century that a long time elapsed before wheeled vehicles came to constitute an important element of road traffic. Goods wagons were mostly for local use. Passenger vehicles had been introduced in the fifteenth century but were largely restricted to the paved streets of cities. By the end of the sixteenth century stage-wagons, carrying passengers as well as goods, were plying between some main centres, but only in summer. They never covered more than twenty miles a day, and that remained the accepted speed for a long time. When the Habsburg Emperor Charles VI visited England in 1703 his fifty-mile journey from London to Petworth in Sussex took three days and the coach turned over a dozen times. Local labourers had to be hired to walk beside it to hold it upright and manhandle it through the muddy patches. There were in fact many parts of Britain where such vehicles could be used only in the best weather. Since the condition of the roads was related to the nature of the soil, in clay country they became impassable when it was wet. London was sometimes almost cut off from the north of England by the belt of clay stretching across the Midlands.

As far back as the Middle Ages there had been a rudimentary system for keeping roads in repair. A surveyor of highways was appointed for each parish with the power to call on local labour to work on the roads during a given number of days in each year. Supervision of the system was supposed to be in the hands of the magistracy, but in few localities was it effective. There were subsequent attempts to regulate road maintenance on a nationwide basis; for example a statute of 1563, in the reign of Queen Elizabeth, which defined the duties of the magistracy more strictly. Comprehensive legislation dealing with road maintenance was not brought forward until the reign of George III. It was consolidated in the General Highways Act of 1835, defining the status and responsibilities of the highway surveyors, a piece of legislation that was not superseded until the end of the nineteenth century.

In the meantime, however, while the condition of the roads, and of the bridges that carried them over rivers, generally remained as poor as the instances quoted above will have indicated, on a number of major routes carrying a quantity of traffic Turnpike Trusts were formed to finance road building and improvement. The first was set up in 1663, and no less than 498 Turnpike Acts were passed between 1720 and 1772. The turnpike system, or at least its economic effectiveness, was marred by the peculation for which toll-collectors soon became notorious, but turnpike roads did at last make it possible for wheeled vehicles of all kinds, including stage coaches and eventually mail coaches (these first ran in 1784 between London and Bristol) to travel with safety and regularity, in winter as well as in summer and at a reasonable speed. Travel became an enjoyable activity rather than an ordeal. The newly surfaced roads ushered in the age of travel for pleasure – of the coaching inn, of country-house visiting, of tourism (for example to Bath and the other watering places that forthwith assumed their peculiar place in the life of fashionable society) and of much else that we associate especially with the Georgian and early Victorian epochs.

Many new bridges at this time were granted rights of toll by Act of Parliament, by means of which the money borrowed to build them by the local (borough or county) authorities was eventually repaid. Since the money the tolls brought in depended on the volume of traffic, towns were able to afford more imposing and substantial bridges than country districts. Better roads and bridges also contributed to the process of rapidly increasing trade between towns and cities that was to be further accelerated in due course by the development of the railways.

Another step forward of lasting significance was taken in 1810 when the Government intervened in actual road construction, chiefly owing to the need to improve communications with Ireland following the Act of Union of 1801. So bad were the Welsh roads in particular that even horse-riders had difficulty in making their way along them. The Government therefore set up a Holyhead Road Commission and appointed Thomas Telford, the son of a Scottish shepherd – the self-taught professional man was characteristic of this era – as its surveyor. As surveyor to the earlier Highland Road Commission Telford was already engaged with notable success in building roads and bridging rivers to open up hitherto inaccessible parts of the Scottish Highlands. For, in spite of the rest of Britain's economic progress, the Highlands had remained a poor and backward region with communications but little improved since General Wade had pushed his military roads through some of the wildest areas a couple of generations earlier.

From 1801 onwards Telford gave Scotland 920 miles of new roads and several hundred new bridges. Of the latter the best known are those at Dunkeld (page 60) and Craigellachie (page 88). His bridge at Dunkeld exemplifies both the variety of motivation and the sense of achievement that animated bridge building at this time. In their report the Commissioners wrote of it:

> The bridge, which has superseded the ancient ferry over the River Tay at Dunkeld, is a magnificent edifice ... and altogether worthy of the grandeur of its situation. The amount of money expended on it, and in opening and forming suitable approaches, is supposed to have exceeded £30,000; the larger portion of which was defrayed by the Duke of Athol, in expectation of a partial remuneration from tolls ... A considerable object was thus attained, Dunkeld being, as it were, the portal of the central Highlands, and more remotely the access to all the northern roads.

Telford's London–Holyhead road, begun in 1817, took twenty years to build. When completed it was in effect Britain's first arterial road. Other enterprises of a similar kind were soon contemplated, for example a rebuilding and re-routing of the Great North Road between London and Edinburgh, for which Telford actually began a survey in 1827, but public enthusiasm for more national highways, and the availability of the capital for their construction, were overtaken by even greater enthusiasm, from the 1830s onwards, for the newly invented railways.

One of Telford's significant initiatives was to design roads with wheeled traffic in mind; until his time the prevailing notion was that the design of vehicles should be adjusted to suit the roads. He insisted on the importance of

Bewdley, Hereford and Worcester. Over the Severn. 1795. By Thomas Telford. See p. 45.

The Serpentine Bridge, Hyde Park, London. 1824. By George Rennie. See p. 47.

Ovingham, Northumberland. Packhorse bridge over the Whittle Burn. Late seventeenth century. See p. 49.

See p. 49.

Aberfeldy, Tayside. Over the Tay. One of the bridges built for General Wade. 1733. By William Adam. See p. 60.

See p. 60.

easy bends and gradients. For horsemen and pack-animals the gradient of a road had not been so important as the need to travel on the higher ground and so avoid water-logged valleys. Only when long-distance coaches and carriages emerged as the regular mode of travel were steep hills regarded as a nuisance. One other factor that made Telford's roads such a big step forward was the contribution of his contemporary John McAdam, a surveyor who laboured to improve the physical process of building roads, the materials used, the method of drainage and the like. As proof of his success his name entered the English language. McAdam was appointed a Highway Surveyor in 1816 and collaborated closely with Telford as well as re-laying many existing roads.

Largely as a result of the initiative of these two men, in the second decade of the nineteenth century Britain began to equip herself – for the first time since the Romans – with well-made trunk roads on which vehicles could travel safely and expeditiously in all weathers, roads of which well-made bridges were an essential part. These were not superseded until the crowding of the roads by petrol-driven vehicles in the middle of the twentieth century demanded a whole new system of motorways and bridges – see Chapter 9.

The Industrial Revolution depended greatly on transport, which would have been impossible without the bridges by which Telford's new highways crossed rivers and their valleys and even arms of the sea; for one of his triumphs, a vital part of the road from London to Holyhead, was his crossing of the Menai Strait to Anglesey by means of a great suspension bridge, completed in 1826. Suspension bridges constitute a category of their own and have so consistently led the way in the development of long-span bridges, from Telford's day right up to the present, that they are accorded a separate chapter in this book. Telford was at the same time a pioneer in the use of iron for bridge building and iron bridges are likewise dealt with in another chapter.

Thus Telford, who had an eye for architectural style to add to his structural inventiveness, became one of history's leading designers of bridges as well as a surveyor and planner of highways, and so did many other of the eminent civil engineers already referred to. Among the most notable of these were John Smeaton, designer also of the Eddystone lighthouse – the versatility of these early engineers was extraordinary – John Rennie, who in 1811 designed London's Waterloo Bridge, demolished in the face of prolonged public protests in 1938, Robert Stevenson (1772–1850), another Scot, better known perhaps as a builder of harbours and lighthouses and the grandfather of the writer Robert Louis Stevenson, and of course Robert Stephenson (1803–59) and Isambard Kingdom Brunel (1806–59), the great railway engineers. The canals, in the building of which Telford was pre-eminent, and the railways created a need to construct a whole new range of bridges with a new and different role. These, like iron bridges and suspension bridges, must be left to another chapter.

A Selection of Notable Bridges of the Seventeenth, Eighteenth and Early Nineteenth Centuries, listed by Counties (by Regions in Scotland)

ENGLAND

Avon

Bath   Pulteney Bridge over the Avon. 1769. By Robert Adam (1728–92). Stone. Three segmental arches, partly rebuilt 1803 after one pier had subsided. Lined with houses mostly now converted to lock-up shops. These and their windows overlooking the river subsequently much altered.

Bedfordshire

Bedford over the Ouse   1811. By John Wing (1756–1826) – see inscription on the parapet. Wing was a prominent local mason-architect who built much in

Pulteney Bridge, Bath, Avon. Over the Avon. 1769. By Robert Adam.

Newbury, Berks. Over the Kennet in the centre of the town. 1769. By James Clarke.

the county. Portland stone. Five segmental arches, the widest central one having a span of 45 feet, and a panelled and balustraded parapet. Replaced a bridge built from the stones of Bedford Castle when this was demolished in 1224. Celia Fiennes, when she crossed the latter bridge in 1698, wrote in her journal, 'At the entrance to the town you pass over the river on a bridge which has a gate on it and some houses'. One of these is believed to have been the house in which John Bunyan was imprisoned while writing part of *Pilgrim's Progress*.

Berkshire

Maidenhead over the Thames 1772. By Sir Robert Taylor. Replaced a wooden bridge. Portland stone. Seven semi-circular arches (the centre one of 33-foot span and the others diminishing in span towards the banks) plus smaller dry arches. Rusticated voussoirs, dentilled cornice and balustraded parapet.

Newbury over the Kennet, in the centre of the town The bridge which replaced a wooden bridge links Northbrook Street and Bridge Street. 1769. By James Clarke, a local master-builder who was also responsible for the 1742

41

town hall (demolished 1908) and for the Dower House. Single elliptical stone arch of 20-foot span with alternate long and short voussoirs. Balustraded parapet. Brick spandrels.

Sonning over the main stream of the divided Thames 1773. Designer unknown. Replaced a wooden bridge said to have existed in Saxon times and mentioned by Leland in 1530. Brick. Eleven semi-circular arches of varying spans. Steep rise towards the centre. The capital to build it was subscribed by a group of local landowners.

Cheshire

Chester Grosvenor Bridge over the Dee. 1827. By Thomas Harrison. One segmental arch, when it was built the largest stone arch in the world – a 200-foot span. Square abutments with niches crowned by pediments. Semi-circular land-arches.

Grosvenor Bridge, Chester. Over the Dee. 1827. By Thomas Harrison.

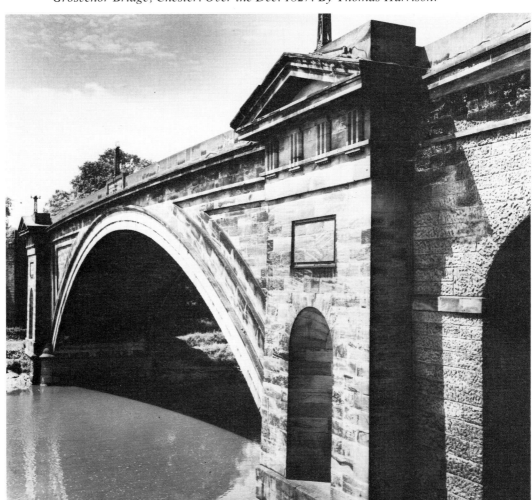

Lanercost, Cumbria. Over the Irthing. 1724.

Cumbria

Lanercost over the Irthing (near Hadrian's Wall)   1724. Replaced a wooden bridge which had fallen down many years previously. There were several fruitless attempts to persuade the Cumberland Justices to order the building of a new bridge and arguments about exactly where it should be sited. As early as 1704 the Justices had been sent a petition by the parishioners of Lanercost supported by those of neighbouring Brampton, which declared that:

> To have a bridge over the River Irthing att the Abby where the old wood Bridge antiently was will not only be of the most use and convenience for the Country and the Markett of Brampton but of the most Safety to stand & without the Charge of Purchaseing any way to itt, the old way being yet open which will be Convenient for all the Inhabitants before mentioned & for the Catle and other Goods which comes Daily to Brampton Markett out of Scotland & the Borders of England.

Nevertheless it was not until 1722 that the Quarter Sessions ordered money to be raised 'for repairinge Abbey Leonard Coast Bridge'. The work was eventually done by four local masons assisted (presumably to erect the centering) by two Whitehaven carpenters. The same four masons were afterwards (according to the *Transactions* of the Cumberland and Westmorland Archaeological Society) appointed to maintain the public bridges throughout the county. Lanercost Bridge is of stone, hump-backed with two partly elliptical and partly segmental arches of 67-foot span and with prominent cutwaters.

Longtown over the Esk   1756. Stone. Five elliptical arches of 50-foot span. Triangular cutwaters with sloping tops.

Newby over the Leven near the southern edge of Lake Windermere   1652. Replaced an earlier bridge. Repaired 1691. By a local builder, Edward Robinson. Slate. Five segmental arches. Pedestrian refuges in prominent cutwaters.

Derbyshire

Bakewell   Holme Bridge over the Wye. Packhorse bridge less than 4 feet wide. 1664. Stone. Five segmental arches plus two small semi-circular arches. Cutwaters with refuges.

Rowsley over the Derwent (not far from Haddon Hall)   Early seventeenth century (widened 1925 and strengthened with mass concrete, but still stone-faced). Five pointed arches with cutwaters.

Devonshire

Totnes over the Dart   1826. By Charles Fowler (1792–1867). Stone. Three rusticated arches.

Dorset

Bishop's Caundle (south-east of Sherborne)   Higher Wood Bridge over Caundle Brook. Late eighteenth century. Local limestone. Four segmental arches on tall narrow piers.

Wimborne   Julian Bridge over the Stour. 1636 (inscription on parapet). Restored 1844 and widened on both sides. Eight pointed arches; seven in stone, one, a replacement, in brick.

Durham

Greta Bridge near Barnard Castle over the Greta   1773 (built after the flood of 1771 had swept away an earlier bridge). By John Carr (1723–1807) who was for thirty years Surveyor of Bridges to the North Riding of Yorkshire. One gracefully Classical stone arch of 75-foot span with roundels in the haunches and niches in the abutments; balustraded parapets slightly bowed. The bridge is the subject of a well-known painting by John Sell Cotman.

Essex

Chelmsford   Moulsham Bridge over the Can. 1787. By John Johnson (1732–1814), a local architect who also designed Chelmsford's Shire Hall. Single segmental brick arch faced with Portland stone. Bowed and balustraded parapet. Johnson served as County Surveyor of Essex and designed several other bridges in the county, of minor interest and now mostly demolished.

Gloucestershire

Bourton-on-the-Water   1806. Replaced first a Roman bridge, then a medieval stone bridge of 1483; widened 1959. Stone. Three low segmental arches. The village has two other small but attractive bridges (see page 163).

Gloucester   Westgate Bridge over the Severn. 1814. Rebuilding of an earlier bridge. By Sir Robert Smirke (1780–1867). Stone. Single arch of 87-foot span.

Hereford and Worcester

Bewdley over the Severn   1795. Replaced a bridge of 1447 destroyed in a flood. By Telford. Sandstone. Three main segmental arches, the widest of 60-foot span, and four flood arches. Prominent voussoirs. Balustraded parapets.

Wilton Bridge over the Wye south-west of Ross-on-Wye   1597. Red sandstone. Five semi-circular ribbed arches. Boldly projecting cutwaters sloping upwards to support pedestrian refuges.

Humberside

Stamford Bridge over the Derwent, near the site of a Roman bridge   1723. Stone. One large segmental arch flanked by semi-circular arches.

Eynsford, Kent. Over the Darent. Seventeenth century.

Kent

Bridge (a village between Canterbury and Dover) over the Stour　Late eighteenth century. Brick with stone keystones to the two segmental arches.

Eynsford over the Darent　Seventeenth century. Kentish ragstone with some brick. Two low round arches with cutwater between.

Newenden over the Rother　1706 (inscription on parapet). Stone. Replaced a medieval bridge. In 1365 a commission was appointed to discover who was responsible for the repair of the bridge 'now long broken … the ferry takes customers to the singular profit of the lord of the boat'.

Lancashire

Lancaster　Skerton Bridge over the Lune. 1783. By Thomas Harrison. Stone. Five elliptical arches with rounded cutwaters surmounted by pedimented niches which pierce right through the piers between the arches. Said to have been the first large bridge with a completely level roadway.

46

London

Hyde Park Serpentine Bridge. 1824. By George Rennie (1791–1866), the eldest son of the more famous John Rennie. Stone. Five segmental arches with scrolled keystones. Small land arches. Balustraded parapet.

Norfolk

Mayton Bridge over the Bure (between Aylsham and Coltishall) Probably seventeenth century. Brick. Two four-centred arches.

Norwich Blackfriars Bridge. 1793. By Sir John Soane (1753–1837). Single stone arch. Widened in early nineteenth century and cast-iron railing added.

Wiggenhall St Mary over the Middle Level Main Drain 1845. Timber (oak framed piers and Danzig fir decking). Seven 3-foot spans.

Northamptonshire

Desborough over the Ise 1780. Stone. Two semi-circular arches with half-round cutwater between; the wing-walls curving gracefully outwards.

Skerton Bridge, Lancaster. Over the Lune. 1783. By Thomas Harrison.

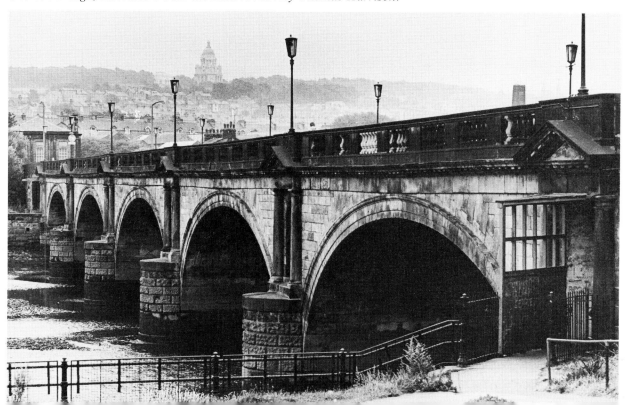

Geddington over the Ise 1784 (reconstruction of a medieval bridge). Local stone. Four arches, three pointed and one semi-circular, with unusually large cutwaters between. Traffic diverted over a new bridge when village bypassed in 1925.

Northumberland

Alnwick Lion Bridge over the Aln. 1773. Replaced a bridge swept away in the floods of 1771. By John Adam (1721–92). Local sandstone. Three semi-circular arches. Battlemented parapets surmounted in centre by sculptured lion (emblem of the Percy family) after which the bridge is named. Painted by Turner, who included bridges in many of his landscapes.

Berwick-on-Tweed Old Bridge over the Tweed, leading to Scotland. 1610. Successor of several earlier bridges, all of wood, including one swept away by floods in 1191, another demolished by the Scots in 1345 and a Tudor bridge swept away by floods and ice in 1608. Sandstone. Fifteen slightly pointed arches, the largest with a span of 75 feet.

The Old Bridge, Berwick-on-Tweed. 1610.

The Lion Bridge, Alnwick, Northumberland. Over the Aln. 1773. By John Adam.

Corbridge over the Tyne near the remains of a Roman bridge at the Roman military camp of Corstopitum   1674. Replaced a wooden bridge of 1235 and a medieval stone one. Widened 1880 by corbelling out the parapets. The only bridge in the region to have resisted the great flood of 1771. Stone. Seven segmental arches.

Haydon Bridge over the West Allen, five miles south-west of the village   Known as the Cupola Bridge after a nearby lead-smelting mill. 1778. Sandstone. Three elegantly proportioned segmental arches with projecting keystones. Low rounded cutwaters.

Hexham over the Tyne   1785 (widened 1965). By the county's bridge sur-veyors, William Johnson (died 1795) and Robert Thompson (advised by Robert Mylne) after the 1777 bridge by Smeaton had been destroyed by a flood in 1782; the new bridge however following Smeaton's design. Stone. Two elliptical and seven segmental arches. Blank circles each with four key-stones in the spandrels. Concrete footways added in 1965.

Ovingham over the Whittle Burn near Prudhoe   Packhorse bridge less than 5 feet wide. Late seventeenth century. Stone. Two segmental arches.

49

Nottinghamshire

Clumber over the Poulter on an estate (from which the mansion has gone) that was once part of Sherwood Forest   1798 (widened 1931). Brick. Three segmental arches with niches between and balustraded parapets. Upstream side formed as a dam to create an artificial lake.

Oxfordshire

Henley over the Thames   1781. Replaced a bridge swept away by floods in 1774. By William Hayward (1740–82). Headington stone. Five elliptical arches with balustraded parapet; heads of 'Thames' and 'Isis' carved on the keystones by a Mrs Damer, a cousin of Horace Walpole. Hayward died before the bridge was finished and asked to be buried underneath the centre arch. His grave, and a memorial tablet, are in fact in Henley parish church.

Oxford   Magdalen Bridge over the Cherwell. 1772 (widened 1882). Replaced a succession of bridges going back at least to 1004 and a ferry. Leland refers to 'est bridge over the Charwell' and goes on to say that 'where now the Bridge of Stone is over Charwell, by Magdalen Colledge, was a trajectus or Ferry in Kynge Henry the Third's Days'. By John Gwynn – the only one of his bridges not over the Severn. Stone. Six arches with carved keystones, rusticated pilasters between and balustraded parapets.

Swinford Bridge   Toll-bridge over the Thames. Replaced an ancient ferry. 1777. Built by James Lord, mason of Eynsham, the nearest town. Stone. Nine arches (three main arches with three smaller approach arches on either side). The larger arches have rusticated voussoirs and a balustrade.

Shropshire

Atcham over the Severn   1776. By Gwynn. Stone. Five arches graduated in height giving the bridge steep gradients. The centre arch has a pedimented pedestal over the parapet. Now used by pedestrians only, having been superseded by a modern bridge built alongside it.

Montford over the Severn west of Shrewsbury   1790. By Telford – his first bridge. Stone. Arches with strongly emphasized voussoirs and bold semi-cylindrical cutwaters.

Shrewsbury English Bridge over the Severn. 1769. Replaced several earlier bridges. By Gwynn. Seven arches of Grinshill stone with balustraded parapets. Partly rebuilt 1925 to flatten arched roadway, but Gwynn's architectural detail preserved including carved dolphins on the cutwaters.

Staffordshire

Colwich Wolsey Bridge over the Trent. 1798. By John Rennie. Stone. Three arches.

Surrey

Chertsey over the Thames 1780 (partly rebuilt 1894). By Paine. Purbeck stone. Five arches plus approach arch at either end. Stone and metal balustrade.

Kingston over the Thames 1825 (widened 1914). By Edward Lapidge (1779–1860). Stone. Five elliptical arches.

Richmond over the Thames 1774 (widened 1929). Replaced a ferry. By James Paine and Kenton Couse (1721–90). Portland stone. Five segmental arches. Balustraded parapet. Painted by Turner.

Sussex, East

Bodiam over the Rother (near Bodiam Castle) 1796. Brick. Three segmental arches with stone keystones.

Warwickshire

Hunningham over the Avon 1651. Reconstruction of a medieval bridge. Stone – very massive. Three semi-circular arches.

Stoneleigh Abbey (near Kenilworth) Sowe Bridge over the Avon. 1814. By John Rennie. Stone. Eight segmental arches.

Warwick Castle Bridge over the Avon. 1789. Replaced earlier bridge 200 yards downstream. By William Eborall (died 1795). Grey sandstone. Single arch of 105-foot span.

Wiltshire

Amesbury   Queensberry Bridge over the Avon. 1775 (inscription on upstream parapet). Stone. Five segmental arches with solid parapets.

Yorkshire, North

Barden (near Bolton Abbey) over the Wharfe   1659. Repaired 1676 after its predecessor, according to local records, had been 'overturned by a wonderful inundation of waters in the northern parts' in 1673. Stone. Three segmental arches with refuges over the cutwaters.

Kexby over the Derwent (east of York where it forms the boundary with Humberside)   1650. Replaced a stone bridge mentioned by Leland and itself little different from local medieval bridges. Stone. Three segmental arches with triple rings.

Richmond over the Swale   1789. Replaced a toll-bridge swept away in the floods of 1771. By Carr. Gatherley Moor stone. Three arches. As Surveyor of Bridges to the North Riding Carr designed several others in the area.

Stainforth, near Settle   Packhorse bridge over the Ribble. Seventeenth century. Stone. Single segmental arch, hump-backed. Belongs to the National Trust.

York   Ouse Bridge. 1810. By Peter Atkinson the younger (1776–1843). Stone. Three elliptical arches. Niches in piers.

WALES

Anglesey

Aberffraw over the Ffraw   1731. Supplemented an ancient ford. Single elliptical arch of 30-foot span. Dry-laid rubble stone, only the ring of the arch being of dressed stone. Now for pedestrians only – traffic diverted to new bridge 1931.

Clwyd

Bangor-is-y-Coed over the Dee south-east of Wrexham   1658. Reputed (erroneously) to be by Inigo Jones. Red sandstone. Five handsomely regular arches. Inscription (largely worn away) giving date of construction, supposed date since the creation of the world (5607) and date since the Muslim *hegira* (1036).

Dyfed

Cardigan over the Teifi   Replaced a medieval bridge. Stone. Five round arches emphatically ringed. Cutwaters between.

Cenarth over the Teifi   Exact date unknown. Three stone arches of 36-foot span.

Llandovery   Dolau-herian Bridge over the Towy. 1773. By William Edwards, the famous Welsh bridge designer. Single segmental stone arch of 84-foot span with circular holes in haunches to lighten the structure. Stone in parapet giving the date and the name of Thomas Edwards, William's son, who no doubt assisted his father.

Cardigan, Dyfed. Over the Teifi.

Pontypridd, Glamorgan. Over the Taff. 1750. By William Edwards.

Lechryd over the Teifi south-east of Cardigan   1656 (inscribed stone). Local stone. Six river arches – very low; bridge completely submerged in flood season.

Pont-ar-Gothi over the Gothi between Carmarthen and Llandeilo   Exact date not known but later than 1675 when a wooden bridge is recorded at this point. Stone. Three segmental arches.

Glamorgan

Pontypridd over the Taff   1750. By William Edwards – his first bridge. Replaced two earlier bridges by the same architect both of which collapsed; the first (1746) from the pressure of trees carried down the river in a flood, the

54

second from faulty construction. Stone. Single arch of 140-foot span – the widest in Britain for the following forty years – very thin at the crown and with holes through the haunches to lighten the structure and avoid another collapse. This became a favourite device of Edwards's and one that was frequently copied, especially in Wales. Pontypridd Bridge is so steeply humped that the adjoining ford was still used until the mid-nineteenth century. It is now stepped. The town was Edwards's birthplace and he is buried there.

Gwent

Monmouth over the Wye   1617 (widened 1879). Stone. Five segmental arches between tall piers with cutwaters.

Pant-y-Goytre over the Usk near Abergavenny   1821. By John Upton of Gloucester who planned the fortifications of Sebastopol. Stone. Three elliptical arches with circular holes in the abutments and over the piers, following the precedent set by William Edwards – see above.

Gwynedd

Llanrwst   Pont Fawr over the Conway. 1636 (westermost of the arches rebuilt 1703). Reputedly by Inigo Jones but this is unlikely. Local shale with sandstone parapets. Cutwaters forming pedestrian refuges. At its western end stands Tu Hwnt i'r Bont, a fifteenth-century courthouse.

Powys

Crickhowell over the Usk   Sixteenth or seventeenth century (widened 1810). Stone. Eight segmental arches with cutwaters, plus five land arches at western end.

SCOTLAND

Borders

Coldstream over the Tweed   1763 (widened 1960). By Smeaton. Sandstone.

Tongueland Bridge, Dumfries and Galloway. Over the Dee. 1804. By Thomas Telford.

Five segmental arches with circular apertures between each, filled with rubble masonry. The arches are of different span and height but their curves are of identical radius, allowing the same centering to be used during construction – an economy pioneered by Smeaton.

Kelso over the Tweed   1799. By John Rennie. Five stone semi-elliptical arches of 72-foot span. Each pier decorated with twin Doric pilasters. Said by Samuel Smiles, in his *Lives of the Engineers*, to have been a model for the same designer's Waterloo Bridge, London (1811; demolished 1938).

Central

Stirling over the Forth (for traffic formerly carried by the Auld Brig of Stirling – see Chapter 1)   1829. By Stevenson. Dressed whinstone. Five segmental arches, the largest central arch having a span of 60 feet.

Dumfries and Galloway

Annan over the Nith   1834. By Stevenson. Stone. Three segmental arches.

Auld Girth over the Nith south of Thornhill   1780. Three stone arches of 56-foot span with pilastered piers supporting pedestrian refuges.

Gilnockie over the Esk near Langholm   1800. Stone. Two large semi-circular arches, the centre one over the main stream unusually handsome. Pedestrian refuges.

Tongueland over the Dee   1804. By Telford in his picturesque castellated style. Annan stone. A single segmental arch, very high because of the steep river-banks and a 20-foot rise of the tide. 112-foot span between rounded abutments. Pointed archways in the wing-walls. Battlemented parapets. The first bridge in which Telford used hollow spandrels to reduce the weight of the arches.

Grampian

Bridge of Dye carrying the Banchory–Montrose road over the Water of Dye Late seventeenth century. Stone. One bold semi-circular arch of 43-foot span between triangular abutments.

Keith over the Isla   1609. Single stone arch.

Bridge of Dye, Grampian. Over the Water of Dye. Late seventeenth century.

Lothian

Cramond Old Bridge over the Almond. 1619 but many times repaired (inscribed stone above the arch). Stone, with one central and two side spans.

Edinburgh Dean Bridge over the Water of Leith. 1829. By Telford. Craigleith stone. Four high (90-foot) segmental arches, each with an inset semi-circular arch.

Edinburgh Regent Bridge over Waterloo Place, the eastern approach to Princes Street. 1815. By Archibald Elliot (1760–1823). Stone. A single arch 50 feet high carrying an open Ionic screen with, in the centre, a Corinthian archway bearing an inscribed panel recording the erection of the bridge.

Regent Bridge, Edinburgh. Over Waterloo Place. 1815. By Archibald Elliot.

Dean Bridge, Edinburgh. Over the Water of Leith. 1829. By Thomas Telford.

Ford over the Tyne Water near Pathhead 1831. By Telford. Stone. Five segmental arches. Similar to the same designer's Dean Bridge at Edinburgh.

Musselburgh over the Esk 1809 (widened 1924). By John Rennie. Stone. Five segmental arches with niched piers between. Three more bridges can be seen from it, one sixteenth-century and the other two modern.

Strathclyde

Glasgow Victoria Bridge over the Clyde. 1851. By James Walker, ironfounder of Rotherham, Yorkshire. The handsomest (and the oldest surviving) of the line of bridges in the centre of the city. Sandstone faced with Irish granite. Five flat segmental arches, the centre one widest with a span of 80 feet.

59

Roadway 80 feet wide, one of the widest in Britain though considerably less than that of Blackfriars Bridge, London (page 179).

Inveraray   New bridge over the Aray. 1774. Reputedly by Robert Adam, perhaps because he designed a Gothic bridge near by which collapsed in 1772; more likely by Robert Mylne. Stone. Two segmental arches with a large circular aperture over the cutwater between. Balustraded parapets.

Tayside

Aberfeldy over the Tay   1733. By William Adam (1689–1748). Built for General Wade as part of his scheme for opening up the Highlands, following the Jacobite rebellion, by means of a system of military roads. Stone. Five segmental arches, the centre one having a 62-foot span. Parapets over central piers crowned by obelisks. Sloping parapets over side arches. This was the next to last of the thirty-five bridges built for General Wade and by far the grandest. It cost more than half his total expenditure on bridges.

Dunkeld over the Tay   1806. By Telford. Replaced an ancient ferry. Five round stone arches plus two smaller land arches. 446 feet long. The bridge is probably unique in having been built, as the poet Robert Southey, who was a friend of Telford's and accompanied him on some of his journeys through Scotland, records in his diary 'on dry ground, formerly the bed of the river; for the Braan which enters a little above the town had brought down gravel enough to force the Tay out of its old channel. When the Bridge was completed the original bed was cleared and made a channel again.'

Montrose   Bridge of Dun over the South Esk west of Montrose Basin. 1785. By Alexander Stevens (1730–96) who designed a number of Scottish bridges. Stone. Three segmental arches. Clusters of columns over the cutwaters supporting pedestrian refuges; pyramids over the abutments and strange incised decorations on the wing-walls.

3

Private and Ornamental Bridges

Before we leave the eighteenth century to embark on the history of the dramatic and unprecedented changes in bridge design which took place in the nineteenth as an outcome of the Industrial Revolution, there is one eighteenth-century phenomenon, as yet hardly touched upon, that requires a chapter to itself. This is the practice, limited to the parks and gardens of country houses, of building bridges for the adornment of the landscape as much as for the fulfilment of practical needs.

The landscaped park, as a setting for a country mansion, enthusiastically adopted in England from the first quarter of the eighteenth century onwards, represented a revolutionary change from the preceding stiff and formal style of garden design with its geometrically-laid-out parterres. The change had been anticipated to some extent by Sir John Vanbrugh (1664-1726) at Castle Howard, begun in 1700. The planting of forest trees by landowners in their private parks had started before this for the wholly practical reason that supplies of timber were becoming scarce owing to the rapid growth of towns and the demands of shipbuilding – John Evelyn was urging landowners to embark on tree-planting as early as 1664. But the real creator of the typically English landscaped park was William Kent (1685-1748), initially a painter though afterwards a distinguished architect, who had studied in Italy during 1709-19 and been captivated by the countryside near Rome and by Italian painters' interpretation of it. The many aristocratic Englishmen who made the Grand Tour were similarly captivated, and especially by the idealized classical landscapes shown in the paintings of Claude and Poussin and the wilder romantic landscapes of Salvator Rosa. They learnt to see nature through such painters' eyes and the latter's translation of nature into a planned composition became the model not only for country-house gardens but for the whole prospect as seen from the house and its surrounding parks and gardens, which the Enclosure legislation, first enacted in 1701, helped to bring under the landowner's control.

61

The first step in the process of creating a picture out of the total landscape was the invention of the ha-ha or sunken fence which allowed the park to be extended visually into the further distance. The ha-ha was introduced by the Royal gardener Charles Bridgman in the garden, now demolished, that he laid out for Lord Burlington at Chiswick in 1717, but it was Kent who first used the device for the creation of unimpeded landscape compositions. In Horace Walpole's words Kent 'leaped the fence and found all nature was a garden'. His first, and very influential, landscaped park was at Rousham, Oxfordshire (1738), where can still be seen the combination of water, skilfully contrived planting and undulating meadowland which were to be the material of the landscapist's art for nearly a hundred years – along with architectural embellishments of various kinds.

Among the last were bridges. There is not, as it happens, a bridge among the ornaments at Rousham except a far older – part thirteenth-, part sixteenth-century – bridge over the Cherwell which Kent incorporated into the entrance to the park but which really belongs to the adjoining village of Heyford (a village so named because it grew up before this bridge existed at a ford used by the hay wagons). However, nearly all the landscaped parks that followed Rousham, whether by Kent's successor Lancelot (known as 'Capability') Brown (1715–83), the most celebrated of all the creators of the 'improved' landscape, or by Humphry Repton (1752–1818), who became the fashionable practitioner of the art after Brown's death and introduced greater naturalness into the scenes which Brown had almost standardized into a formula, contained bridges; for an essential ingredient of their design was water, and bridges were needed to provide a way across it.

The water took the form of a stream or river, more often than not widened into a lake. William Shenstone (1714–63), both a poet and one of the pioneers of the picturesquely-laid-out garden, wrote in his posthumously published essay on gardening (1765), 'The eye should always look down upon water; customary nature makes this requisite.' The water contributed liveliness to the prospect and romantically reflected the groups of trees – Capability Brown's notorious 'clumps' – as well as the many other embellishments sited round the margins of the lakes which provided the focal points of cunningly contrived views and were sometimes given additional movement and sparkle by a cascade. Bridges took the visitor across the stream or the narrower arms of the lake, allowing him to progress along the system of paths which were not only a convenience but were necessary to the purpose of the design, since this was conceived as something to be appreciated from a moving viewpoint, to unfold itself to the visitor as he pursued his way round the park or garden; and the winding path, assisted on its way by bridges and punctuated by seats, was planned so as to ensure that the views were enjoyed from the most effective points and in the most desirable succession. Jean-Jacques Rousseau, an early

French admirer of the charms of the English landscaped garden, wrote in *La Nouvelle Héloïse* (1760) that its walks should be 'somewhat irregular, like the steps of an indolent man'.

The bridges that served this practical purpose were conceived also as adornments of the landscape. They may have played a minor part compared with the many other architectural embellishments that Kent and his successors introduced – temples and grottoes, urns and obelisks – some being major works of architecture in their own right, such as Hawksmoor's mausoleum at Castle Howard, but most being little more than eye-catching incidents. They lie outside the scope of this book but it has been necessary to refer to their origin and purpose, and to the nature of the landscape movement, in order to make clear the picturesque as well as the functional role of the bridges that are numbered among them.

Bridges not only play a prominent scenic role but they reflect the variety of taste and fashion followed by the designers of parks, the architects of the houses for which they were the setting (sometimes but not often the same individual) and the owners whose initiative caused them to flourish. The rise of the landscaped park, for example, coincided with that of the Palladian style of architecture, and we find imitations of Palladio's own designs introduced into the landscape as in the case of the famous covered bridges at Wilton, Stowe and Prior Park. The more exotic fashions, like the fashion for chinoiserie promoted initially by Sir William Chambers (1723–96) and exemplified in a number of bridges over lakes and streams, and the first romantic stirrings of the Gothic Revival, are to be found in the grottoes and artificial ruins in many landscaped parks although bridges played little part in this movement until later.

Most of the bridges listed at the end of this chapter (as well as a few of the suspension bridges and footbridges in Chapters 7 and 8) were the product of the pleasure taken during the eighteenth century in landscaped parks. Some were built later, but still for the most part as ornaments in the landscape. The vogue for these continued long after the direct influence of the Classical landscape painters and the aspiration to create idyllic scenes inspired by their interpretation of nature had lapsed. Literature had at the beginning been a principal influence on the fashion for picturesque landscaping, but as time went on not all writers continued to express the same enthusiasm, or to approve of the elaborate adornment of parks and gardens by means of architectural features. The invariably down-to-earth John Claudius Loudon, for example, in his *Encyclopaedia of Cottage, Farm and Villa Architecture* published in 1833, extended his criticism even to bridges. He writes in his chapter on Ornamental Garden Structures:

Bridges are among the noblest structures which can be erected in pleasure-grounds; and, unlike rustic seats and root-houses, they maintain this character even when constructed of materials of temporary duration, from their obvious and unquestionable utility. A mere plank or tree, when thrown across a stream, assumes a character of grandeur; it commands respect for its power of effecting for man what he could not, by any possibility, effect for himself. On the other hand, when a trifling stream, or an artificial river, displays a highly architectural bridge of masonry or cast iron, the effect is offensive; because the means seem out of all proportion to the end. In short, a massive highly architectural stone bridge, built across a tame piece of water, not perhaps more than knee-deep, and an elaborate covered seat of rustic cabinet-work, which cannot endure many seasons, offend precisely for the same reason; viz., the unsuitability of means to ends.

A Selection of Notable Private and Ornamental Bridges, listed by Counties (by Regions in Scotland)

ENGLAND

Avon

Prior Park, Bath   Covered stone bridge by the edge of the lake. The second of such 'Palladian' bridges to be built in England, so called because modelled on a much-admired design by Andrea Palladio (1508–80), the Italian architect who by precept and example exercised a dominant influence upon English eighteenth-century architecture. This bridge is almost identical with those at Wilton, Wiltshire (the first) and Stowe, Buckinghamshire - see below. 1755. By John Wood the elder (1704–54) who built the house at Prior Park for Ralph Allen. Allen's clerk of works, Richard Jones, claimed to have designed the bridge, but it is much more likely to have been Wood himself. Combe Down limestone. Ionic colonnade with arches and pedimented end pavilions, supported on a central semi-circular arch and two side arches; additional arches beneath the stepped approaches.

Buckinghamshire

Stowe House   Covered 'Palladian' bridge over the north-east end of the lake.

1742. Similar to the above but copied from the one at Wilton – see below. Ionic colonnade with arched and pedimented end pavilions. Semi-circular arch with two side arches; larger round arches beneath the stepped approaches. The bridge is one of no less than thirty-eight architectural ornaments of various kinds disposed about this beautifully landscaped park by many hands (not in this instance including Lancelot Brown although he was employed at Stowe for thirteen years – 1737–50 – first as garden-boy and eventually as head gardener). The house, now a school, was built for Sir Richard Temple, mostly by Robert Adam (1728–92) and the amateur architect Thomas Pitt (1737–93). Architects of buildings in the park include Vanbrugh, Kent, James Gibbs (1682–1754), Sir Robert Lorimer (1864–1929) and Sir Clough Williams-Ellis (1883–1978).

'Palladian' bridge, Stowe House, Bucks. 1742.

Tyringham Hall 1793. By Sir John Soane. Single-arched hump-backed stone bridge with incised lines after the familiar Soane fashion, and niches in the abutments. The house, also by Soane, was designed in the same year for William Praed.

Cambridgeshire

Wimpole Hall Footbridge in the park, probably built as part of Lancelot Brown's remodelling in 1769–74. Wood on brick piers, with Chinese-style handrail; weir beneath. The bridge has been rebuilt by the National Trust

Tyringham Hall, Bucks. 1793. By Sir John Soane.

incorporating some of the original material. The house is of many periods from 1632 onwards, the larger part designed in 1719 by James Gibbs for Edward Harley, later Earl of Oxford; interior alterations by Soane.

Cheshire

Eaton Hall over the Dee on the east side of the park   1824. Iron. Built for the Earl of Grosvenor by William Hazledine (1763–1840), an ironfounder who supplied ironwork for Telford's Menai and Conway suspension bridges – see Chapter 7. There is a bust of Hazledine by Chantrey in Shrewsbury parish church. Single arch of 150-foot span. Jervoise, writing in 1936, called it 'probably the most elegant iron bridge in existence'. The house was remodelled in 1870–83 by Alfred Waterhouse (1830–1905) for the first Duke of Westminster but demolished in 1961. The park was at least partly the work of the landscape architect John Webb (1754–1828).

Henbury Hall near Macclesfield, over the lake in the park for the use of estate workers and their tractors   1957. By S. Fairhurst and Son. Reinforced concrete deck, slightly arched, supported on two sandstone piers remaining from an earlier bridge. Deck 7 feet wide with, unusually, no parapet; edge marked instead by smooth instead of ribbed concrete. Centre span 11 feet. The house has been demolished; only the eighteenth-century stables are left.

Tatton Park over the lake in the Japanese Garden: footbridge in Japanese style   1910. Wood. One flattish arch. The neo-Classical house was designed by Samuel Wyatt (1737–1807) for William Egerton in 1785 and added to by his nephew Lewis Wyatt (1777–1853) for Wilbraham Egerton in 1807. The layout of the park is largely by Repton, John Webb being consulted also. The Japanese Garden was laid out in 1910 for the third Lord Egerton by Japanese workmen brought over for the purpose, as was the Shinto temple to which the footbridge leads. The house and park now belong to the National Trust.

Cornwall

Trelissick House, Feock, over a public road leading to a ferry across the estuary of the Fal   1824. Probably by P. F. Robinson (1776–1858), the architect of the formal Greek Revival mansion built in the same year for Thomas Daniell. The bridge, which may have been rebuilt around 1860, is of wrought iron with brick parapets capped with granite. The house and gardens belong to the National Trust but only the latter are open to the public.

Derbyshire

Chatsworth House over the Derwent as it flows through the park 1759. By James Paine. Stone. Handsomely Classical with three segmental arches on rusticated piers. Statues on the cutwaters reputed to be by the sculptor C. G. Cibber who made many statues for the gardens at Chatsworth, but this attribution is questionable because Cibber died in 1700. Richly ornamented balustrade. Paine also built, in 1760, a single-arched stone bridge of 66-foot span carrying a public road through the park and known as the Beeley or Edensor Bridge. It is remarkable for having stone ribbing beneath the arch in medieval style. Chatsworth House was built in stages between 1687 and 1841 for successive Dukes of Devonshire, the architects being in turn William Talman (1650–1719), Thomas Archer (1668–1743) and Sir Jeffry Wyatville (1766–1840). The park was laid out by Lancelot Brown who at the same time widened the river which the second of Paine's two bridges crosses.

Dorset

Sherborne Castle   Pinford Bridge in the park. 1790. Supposed to be by Robert Mylne but the Castle Museum has a design for a similar bridge signed by Adam and dated 1767. Stone. Pilastered buttresses between the arches. The

Edensor Bridge, Chatsworth House, Derbyshire. 1760. By James Paine.

'Indian' bridge, Sezincote House, Glos. 1807. By Thomas Daniell.

house is Elizabethan, built for Sir Walter Raleigh in 1594 near the medieval Old Castle and added to in 1617 by Sir John Digby. The park was laid out by Brown who created the lake between the castle and the Elizabethan lodge, which the bridge crosses. The Old Castle was dismantled after the Civil War.

Gloucestershire

Barrington Park   Chinese bridge. 1820. Designer unknown. The Palladian house (1740) is by Henry Joynes (1684–1754) who was Vanbrugh's clerk of works at Blenheim. It was much altered in the nineteenth century.

Sezincote House   Indian bridge carrying the drive north of the park over a stream and valley forming part of the Humphry Repton landscaping. 1807. By Thomas Daniell (1749–1840), the topographical artist who worked principally in India and advised the architect of the house, Samuel Pepys Cockerell (1753–1827), on the use of Indian styles. Stone, with close-set octagonal pillars four deep and pierced stone parapets decorated with bulls in cast iron.

69

Greater London

Osterley Park 'Roman' bridge in the park. 1763–80. Rustic stone. By the brothers Adam who remodelled the Elizabethan house in 1763 for Robert Child the banker. The bridge is now disused and in a ruinous condition. Most of the park (but not the area containing the bridge) belongs to the National Trust. The house is administered by the Victoria and Albert Museum.

Hertfordshire

Cassiobury Park, Watford, over the Grand Junction Canal   A rare instance of a canal bridge in the grounds of a private house. Early nineteenth century. Architect unknown. One high semi-circular arch flanked by pilasters with cornice and balustraded parapet. The house, originally Elizabethan but remodelled in 1674 by Hugh May (1621–84) and in 1800 by James Wyatt (1746–1813) has been totally demolished. The grounds, originally landscaped by Webb, were laid out afresh by Repton in 1801.

London

Ken Wood House on the edge of Hampstead Heath   A dummy bridge, and thus an extreme case of the bridge built solely as an eye-catcher. It appears to be a bridge only when seen across the park from the Robert Adam house (begun 1767) and is in fact no more than an arched wall surmounted by a balustrade. The house and park belong to the Greater London Council.

Northumberland

Cragside House, Rothbury, over the Debdon Burn near the house   Around 1870. Steel footbridge high above a ravine. One main and two approach spans. Total length 150 feet. The bridge was made in the Elswick works of the owner of the house, Lord Armstrong, engineer, inventor and armaments manufacturer. It was designed for him in 1864 by Richard Norman Shaw (1831–1912) in the 'Old English' style typical of the early part of his career. The house and grounds now belong to the National Trust.

Wallington Hall over the Wansbeck   The main approach to the house remodelled for Sir Walter Blackett by Daniel Garrett (died 1753), a protégé of Lord Burlington, between 1735 and 1753. The bridge, added in 1760, is by

Paine. Stone. One elliptical arch over the river, flanked by two land arches. Niches in the square piers between the balustraded parapets. The park was laid out by Lancelot Brown who was born near by. The house and park now belong to the National Trust.

Oxfordshire

Blenheim Palace over the Glyme (now part of the lake formed later by Brown which brought the water-level higher up the bridge)   1708. By Vanbrugh who designed Blenheim for the Duke of Marlborough, 1705–16. Stone. Central segmental arch of 100-foot span; niched piers between. The bridge was unfinished when the work at Blenheim was temporarily halted in 1712 – it was to have been surmounted by turrets and an arcade. The simpler Bladon Bridge of 1773, also in the park, is by Sir William Chambers.

Blenheim Palace, Oxfordshire. 1708. By Sir John Vanbrugh.

Shropshire

Attingham Hall   A public road bridge over the Tern, which was widened here when Repton laid out the park. 1780 (widened 1932). By William Hayward, probably following a design by Mylne who worked for Noel Hill on the earlier house on the site, Tern Hall. The present house was built for the first Lord Berwick in 1783 by George Steuart (1730–1806) and altered in 1807 by John Nash (1752–1835). The house and park now belong to the National Trust.

Staffordshire

Chillington Hall over the canal in the park   1770. By Paine. Stone. Decorated with medallions and niches in the piers. The house was designed for Peter Gifford in 1724 by Francis Smith (1672–1738) and remodelled by Soane in 1785.

Attingham Hall, Shropshire. 1780. By William Hayward.

'Chinese' bridge, Shugborough Park, Staffs. 1813. By Charles Heywood.

Shugborough (see also Chapter 1) Chinese bridge in the park. 1813. By Charles Heywood. Cast iron painted red. The house was begun in 1693 and subsequently added to by several architects including James Stuart (1713–88), and Samuel Wyatt. The park, at least partly laid out by Webb in 1804, is exceptionally rich in architectural ornaments, mostly by Stuart, commissioned by Thomas Anson. The house and park now belong to the National Trust.

73

Weston Park, Weston-under-Lizard   'Roman' bridge. 1765. By Paine. The early Classical house was built in 1671 for Sir Thomas and Lady Wilbraham and is said to have been designed by Lady Wilbraham. The park was laid out, at least in part, by the landscapist Webb in 1827.

Surrey

Pain's Hill House   Suspension bridge over the Portsmouth Road. By Joseph Bramah (1748–1814), inventor and locksmith. The house is by Richard Jupp (1728–99); the garden, much admired by Horace Walpole, was landscaped by its owner Charles Hamilton in the 'savage' style inspired by the paintings of Salvator Rosa.

Weston Park, Staffs. 1765. By James Paine.

Sussex, East

Ashburnham Place over the lake in the park previously (1767) landscaped by Brown   1813. By George Dance the younger (1741–1825). Stone. One segmental arch with tall pedestals over the abutments. Most of the house, the home of the Earl of Ashburnham, was demolished in 1959.

Warwickshire

Charlecote Park over the Wellesbourne Brook   1755. By David Hiorn (died 1758). Stone. One segmental arch with voussoirs emphasized; parapets with square balusters, stopped by pedestals with balls on top. The bridge is peculiar in being more ornamented on the side facing the house. It is near the entrance to the park, which was landscaped by Brown in 1760. The Elizabethan house was built for Sir Thomas Lucy in 1558. It was altered and enlarged in the nineteenth century. The house and park now belong to the National Trust.

Compton Verney over the lake in the park   1770. By Lancelot Brown who landscaped the park and in 1776 added a chapel to the house. Stone. Three segmental arches with niches in the abutments. The house (original architect unknown) was built in 1714 for the twelfth Lord Willoughby de Broke, extended in 1760 by Robert Adam and added to in 1855 by John Gibson (1817–92).

Warwick Castle
OLD BRIDGE   1374. Stone. Six arches with cutwaters.
MYLNE BRIDGE   1765. By the architect of the same name. Grey sandstone. One segmental arch with carved keystone. Balustraded parapet with unusual square pillars.

Wiltshire

Amesbury Abbey   Baluster Bridge north of the house. 1778. By Smeaton – his only Classical design. Stone. Three low elliptical arches. Balustraded parapets. The present house was built in 1834 by Thomas Hopper (1776–1856) for Sir Edmund Antrobus after the latter had pulled down a house of 1661 by John Webb (1611–72).

Stourhead over the end of the lake   1762. Stone. Five segmental arches (modelled on a bridge at Vicenza by Palladio). Also an iron bridge over the south-western arm of the lake. 1860 (replacing a wooden bridge of 1842). By Maggs and Hindley, ironfounders. The house was designed for Henry Hoare in 1721 by Colen Campbell (1676–1729). Its gardens are among the most richly planted in England and the most splendidly adorned with grottoes, temples and all kinds of eye-catchers. The house and gardens now belong to the National Trust.

Wilton House Covered bridge over the Nadder, the earliest of the 'Palladian' bridges – see Prior Park, Avon, and Stowe House, Buckinghamshire. 1736. Probably by Colen Campbell and Roger Morris (1695–1749). Stone. Ionic colonnade with arched and pedimented end pavilions. Semi-circular arch with two side arches, and additional arches under the stepped approaches. It is one of many eighteenth-century architectural ornaments in the park of this house built for the Earl of Pembroke in 1636 under the supervision of Inigo Jones (1573–1652). The Earl may himself have had a hand in the design of the bridge – he supervised the building of Labelye's Westminster Bridge (1739; replaced 1854) – see page 33.

Yorkshire, North

Castle Howard New River Bridge. 1744. Modelled on a design by Palladio and probably the work of Daniel Garrett. Stone. Three arches with bands of rock-faced rustication. Similarly treated keystones, one with a large carved head. Pedimented niches in the spandrels. It is one of many architectural monuments, mostly by Vanbrugh or Hawksmoor, in the park surrounding this great house designed by Vanbrugh for the third Earl of Carlisle between 1700 and 1726 and completed by Sir Thomas Robinson (1702–77) in 1759.

WALES

Powys

Abercamlais near Penpont, over the Usk 1600 (widened 1780 on the up-stream side). Architect unknown. Four stone arches. In the grounds of an early-eighteenth-century house built, like Penpont House close by, for the Williams family.

SCOTLAND

Borders

Bowhill carrying the drive to the house over Ettrick Water   1833. By John Smith (1782–1864) who built both bridge and house for the Duke of Buccleuch.

Dumfries and Galloway

Dumfries House, Cumnock, over Lugar Water at the edge of the park   1760. By John Adam (1721–92). Stone. Three elliptical arches of which the centre one only is topped by an open balustrade with tall obelisks at either end. John Adam had already (1754–9) built the house for the fourth Earl of Dumfries.

Lothian

Dalkeith House   Montagu Bridge, carrying the west drive over the North Esk. 1792. By Robert Adam but completed by his brother James after Robert's

Dumfries House, Dumfries and Galloway. 1760. By John Adam.

death. Stone. A single semi-circular arch. Deep niches in the abutments with panels over them and other Classical embellishments. The house was built in 1702 for the Duchess of Buccleuch by James Smith (1645–1731).

Oxenfoord Castle 1773. By Alexander Stevens. Stone. Three semi-circular arches, castellated above. The old castle, near which the bridge crosses a valley in the park, was rebuilt for Sir John Dalrymple in 1780 by Robert Adam in his romantic castle style and added to in 1840 by William Burn (1789–1870).

Strathclyde

Inveraray Dubh Loch Bridge in the grounds of the old (now ruined) Inveraray Castle. 1786. By Robert Mylne for the fifth Duke of Argyll. Stone. One segmental arch. Solid parapets battlemented over the abutments.

4

Early Iron Bridges

Although bridge building may have become more expert during the centuries covered by the first two chapters of this book, the methods employed changed very little; indeed they were much the same as those used by the Romans who preceded them: basically arches of masonry or brick with the spandrels filled with loose stones, gravel or earth to make a bed on which to lay the roadway. Only with the Industrial Revolution which began late in the eighteenth century were totally new methods introduced. The material that made the Industrial Revolution possible was iron – iron for machines, for bridges, for railways, for the locomotives that ran on them and eventually for the ships that carried the trade the Revolution promoted across the oceans of the world. How sudden an innovation this was is indicated by the fact that until the middle of the eighteenth century two-thirds of Britain's production of iron was used in agriculture.

The building of bridges was one of the first structural uses of iron, preceded only by the columns (but not yet the beams) that supported the floors of the new textile weaving mills. Robert Mylne was mentioned in Chapter 2 as the architect of a number of outstanding eighteenth-century masonry bridges, and he also has the distinction of having designed in 1774 what was almost certainly the first bridge using iron, but it was never built. It was to have been at Inveraray, Strathclyde, using the abutments of the old town bridge which was due to be demolished following the construction of a new bridge over the Aray (also, it is thought, designed by Mylne – see page 60). His pioneer iron bridge was to have had a timber roadway supported on cast-iron ribs forming two arches, with ornamental iron railings in what was then called the Chinese taste. Iron was thought of at this time as a substitute for wood rather than for stone, and Thomas Farnolls Pritchard (1723–77), the son of a joiner who himself began as one before he took up architecture and who practised mostly in Shropshire, made several experimental designs using iron where wood would normally have been used. One of these, made at the end of 1775, was for a bridge wholly of iron over the Severn at a point near Coalbrookdale now called

79

– after the bridge he eventually built – Iron-Bridge. Coalbrookdale was an important centre of the iron-making industry and a leading ironmaster, Abraham Darby (one of a dynasty of Quaker ironmasters who first succeeded in smelting iron with coke instead of charcoal), played a large part in bringing this project to fruition and indeed finalized the design of the bridge after Pritchard's death.

The Coalbrookdale bridge, the world's first iron bridge to be actually built – and it is still standing although, not surprisingly, it has needed several repairs – was begun in 1777 and completed in 1779. Here the roadway, made of iron slag and clay, is supported on iron plates carried across the river on one great cast-iron arch of 100-foot span, formed of five semi-circular ribs braced together at intervals. The ribs are built up of small cast-iron panels shaped like the voussoirs of a stone arch, and the jointing and the dovetailed connections are reminiscent of timber construction. How best to employ iron had not yet therefore been fully worked out. Nevertheless the Coalbrookdale bridge was the beginning of a dramatic step forward leading to the construction of bridges of far greater span than in the past. This was made possible mainly because iron, in due course to be replaced by steel, is strong in tension as well as in

Coalbrookdale (Iron-Bridge), Shropshire. Over the Severn. 1777. By Thomas Pritchard and Abraham Darby.

compression whereas stone and brick are strong only in the latter.

The next experiments with iron for bridges were made not by an architect or engineer or even by an ironfounder but by a political philosopher, Thomas Paine (1737–1809), author of *The Rights of Man*, who in 1788 took out a patent for a new type of iron bridge, segmental in shape with five cast-iron ribs and a span of 110 feet. He in fact built it in 1790 as a temporary demonstration of his method on a bowling-green outside a Paddington public house where it remained for a year, drew large crowds and aroused the interest of many architects and engineers as well as of members of the Royal Society. A variation of Paine's design was built over the Wear at Sunderland between 1793 and 1796. The engineer was Thomas Wilson, who had previously served as agent to James Watt (1736–1819), the scientist and inventor who did so much to improve the steam engine. The ironwork for the Sunderland bridge was cast at the Walker foundry at Rotherham. Some of the parts incorporated in it had been cast there earlier for a bridge Paine had designed to cross the Schuykill River in America but had not been used (no iron bridge was constructed in America until 1836).

The Sunderland bridge had the same five iron ribs, each built up of cast-iron panels, as that at Coalbrookdale. Its spandrels were filled with circular iron hoops and this time the bridge had the unprecedented span of 236 feet, with a rise of 34 feet. It was an achievement so widely admired that engravings of the bridge were used to decorate innumerable household objects such as pottery jars and mugs. It stood until 1858 when it was replaced by a bridge designed by Robert Stephenson. This in its turn was replaced in 1929 by a steel arch bridge – see page 183.

A modification of the Sunderland design, for which a patent was jointly taken out in 1802 by Wilson its engineer and Rowland Burdon, the Member of Parliament for Durham who had been one of its principal promoters, became the basis of a smaller bridge at Newport Pagnell, Buckinghamshire – Tickford Bridge – completed in 1810 and still standing.

In the years after the Sunderland bridge was completed the Coalbrookdale company cast a quantity of iron ribs for small-span bridges – half a rib at each casting – and at least two of these bridges are still in use for foot traffic; one at Cound, Shropshire, and the other at Bath over the Kennet and Avon Canal, both built in 1797. The next developments in bridge-building in iron were the work of two of the great engineers mentioned in Chapter 2: John Rennie and Thomas Telford. Both had already designed important stone bridges, for example Rennie at Kelso, Borders, in 1799 (see page 56) and Telford at Bewdley, Hereford and Worcester, also in 1799 (see page 45) and the seven-arch Broomielaw Bridge at Glasgow which was demolished in 1899. Rennie was to go on to build his most famous bridge, Waterloo Bridge in London (1811–1938), again in stone, but after the turn of the century the inventive powers of both these engineers were to be turned to the enlargement and the more economical construction of iron bridges.

Telford, whose improved highways made him one of the heroes of Chapter 2 of this book and whose giant aqueducts will again make him the hero of Chapter 5, showed boldness as well as expertise when he published a project in 1800 for a new London Bridge to span the Thames by means of a single arch of 600 feet. It was not accepted, but it remains one of the great unexecuted projects of history (see pages 188 and 198). In 1788 he was appointed Surveyor of Public Works for Shropshire and designed forty-two bridges in that county, some in stone and some to a standard design in iron. His first iron bridge was over the Severn at Buildwas (1795), just upstream from Coalbrookdale. Unlike the Coalbrookdale bridge it had a single arch of segmental rather than semi-circular shape. It was 30 feet longer (spanning 130 feet instead of 100 feet) and yet used only 173 tons of iron as against 378 at Coalbrookdale. It was demolished in 1905.

Although confidence in the use of iron was growing there were some setbacks. Thomas Wilson (see preceding page) built a cast-iron bridge over the Thames at Staines in 1803 but it had to be taken down the same year when fractures appeared in the ironwork, and a bridge at Bristol by another engineer, William Jessop (1745-1814; later the engineer of the Grand Junction Canal) collapsed soon after it was built in 1805. The two castings of which its iron ribs were formed (cast at Coalbrookdale) were the heaviest that had yet been tried.

In spite of the caution such occurrences engendered Telford did not hesitate to build occasionally in iron when he worked in Scotland after being appointed in 1803 as engineer to the Highland Road Commission – see Chapter 2. Most of the bridges he built over Highland rivers were of stone, an easily available local material, but when an unusually large-span bridge was required he decided to use iron, for example, over Dornoch Firth, Highland, at Bonar further up the same firth and most successfully at Craigellachie, Grampian, where his bridge over the Spey, with a single span of 150 feet, was completed in 1815. It shows increasing mastery over the new techniques in spite of its abutments being furnished with castellated towers that look backwards towards the old. His confidence in the future of iron was justified when, in 1814, large blocks of ice and heavy tree-trunks were flung violently against his bridge at Bonar in a flood that followed a great storm but caused it no damage.

Telford built a similar bridge over the Esk near Carlisle in 1820 and another over the Severn at Tewkesbury in 1823. The first was demolished in 1916 but the second still stands although carrying only light traffic. A more remarkable bridge was the one he built in 1815 over the Conway at Betws-y-coed, Gwynedd, as part of his London–Holyhead road improvement. It has a single span of 105 feet and is known as the Waterloo Bridge because of the cast-iron

Waterloo Bridge, Betws-y-coed, Gwynedd. Over the Conway. 1815. By Thomas Telford.

inscription commemorating the Battle of Waterloo incorporated in the design – see the list of early iron bridges at the end of this chapter.

The largest cast-iron arch to be built in Britain was by Rennie, who in 1800 had built his first iron bridge, rather more modest in size, at Boston, Lincolnshire. The latter was remarkable for being the first bridge to employ wrought iron instead of cast iron in order to make it lighter. The wrought iron used weighed just over three tons. If cast iron had been used it would, according to Ted Ruddock (see Bibliography), have weighed 208 tons. Rennie's ironwork in this bridge was replaced by steel in 1912. Also in 1800 he built an exceptionally elegant five-arch bridge over the Wye at Chepstow – see again the list at the end of this chapter.

His large-span cast-iron arch bridge, referred to above, was in London: Southwark Bridge, one of three toll-bridges built over the Thames in the space of ten years after 1810, all designed by Rennie. These were Vauxhall, Waterloo and Southwark Bridges. However his design for Vauxhall Bridge, which was to have been of stone, proved too expensive and the directors of the toll company commissioned instead a nine-arch iron bridge from Sir Samuel Bentham (1757–1831) the eminent naval engineer, whose design was subsequently modified by James Walker, the Rotherham ironfounder. It was completed in 1816 and was thus the first iron bridge over the Thames. It was originally called Regent Bridge but its name was soon changed because of its proximity to the highly popular Vauxhall Gardens. It was replaced in 1895 by the present concrete and steel bridge, the first Thames bridge to be crossed by tramcars. Rennie's Waterloo Bridge, also of stone, is well known and has been referred to here already. His Southwark Bridge was designed to have only three arches, but these were of exceptionally wide span to allow the passage of largish ships in case the talked-of rebuilding of London Bridge further down-river should let them up so far – which in fact, after 1831, it did. The segmental arches at Southwark were of iron, supported on stone piers, and the centre arch had a span of 240 feet and rose twenty-four feet above high-tide level. It was originally known simply as 'The Iron Bridge' (Dickens called it so in *Little Dorrit*). It was completed in 1819 and stood until 1921.

A Selection of Notable Early Iron Bridges, listed by Counties (by Regions in Scotland)
(for others see under Canal Bridges pp. 89–106 and Railway Bridges pp. 107–37)

ENGLAND

Avon

Bath   Cleveland Bridge over the Avon from Bathwick. 1827 (reconstructed 1928). By Henry Goodridge (1797–1864). Cast iron. One segmental arch of 100-foot span consisting of six parallel ribs with latticed spandrels. Heavy pierced iron railing. The bridge has stone abutments above which stand toll-houses in the form of small Doric temples with pedimented porticoes.

Buckinghamshire

Newport Pagnell   Tickford Bridge over the Lovat near its junction with the

Ouse. 1810. By a little-known Paddington architect, Henry Provis, Surveyor to the Grand Junction Canal Company (his son, William Alexander Provis, 1792–1870, became Telford's first and most valued assistant and resident engineer during the construction of Telford's Menai and Conway suspension bridges – see Chapter 7. He was afterwards a railway engineer). Henry Provis was assisted by William Yates, an employee of the Walker ironfoundry at Rotherham who had been foreman during the construction of Sunderland Bridge and later assisted Rennie with the details of his Southwark Bridge over the Thames. Cast iron from the Walker foundry. Single flattish arch composed of six ribs connected by horizontal straps. Both the arch-rings and the spandrels, which are formed of two separate castings, are ornamented with arrangements of circles. Abutments of local stone. The iron bridge replaced an old stone bridge which had itself replaced a wooden bridge, some of the remains of which were found when the foundations of the abutments of the iron bridge were being dug. That iron as a material for bridges was still doubtfully regarded by some in 1810 is shown by the following extract from the minutes (preserved in the Buckinghamshire county archives) of a meeting of the bridge trustees held at the Swan Inn, Newport Pagnell, on 6th February of that year: 'That the Thanks of this meeting be given to Mr. Cautley' (the Revd Richard Cautley, one of the trustees) 'for the trouble he has taken in going a Journey to Sunderland in order to procure information respecting the plans and construction of Iron Bridges in different situations, and the comparative Expence and convenience of Stone and Iron Bridges.' For the bridge he went to look at see page 81.

Devonshire

Exeter over a valley at the end of North Street, built to eliminate the steep descent and ascent of one of the main roads into the city (the valley originally contained the Long Brook, already covered over)   1834. Cast iron. Built by the Blaina ironfoundry, Gwent. Designer unknown. Six arches each of 40-foot span supported on sturdy cast-iron columns. Continues as a stone causeway. Total length 800 feet.

Gloucestershire

Tewkesbury   Mythe Bridge over the Severn. 1823. By Telford. A single arch of 174-foot span with delicate cross-bracing. Stone abutments pierced by tall narrow Gothic arches designed to lighten the appearance and to disperse flood-water.

Norfolk

Letheringsett over the Glaven   1818. By William Hardy. Cast iron. Iron railings with unusual large flat balusters.

Norwich   Fye Bridge. 1829. By Francis Stone (1775–1835), a local architect who was County Surveyor from 1806 until his death. He also built an iron bridge at Thetford (1829) as well as a number of other bridges in the county. In 1830 he published a set of lithographs entitled *Picturesque Views of All the Bridges belonging to the County of Norfolk*.

Shropshire

Atcham over the Shropshire Union Canal   1818. By Telford. Cast iron. Segmental arch and slender iron railing.

Coalbrookdale (Iron-Bridge) over the Severn   1777 – the world's first iron

Atcham, Shropshire. Over the Shropshire Union Canal. 1818. By Thomas Telford.

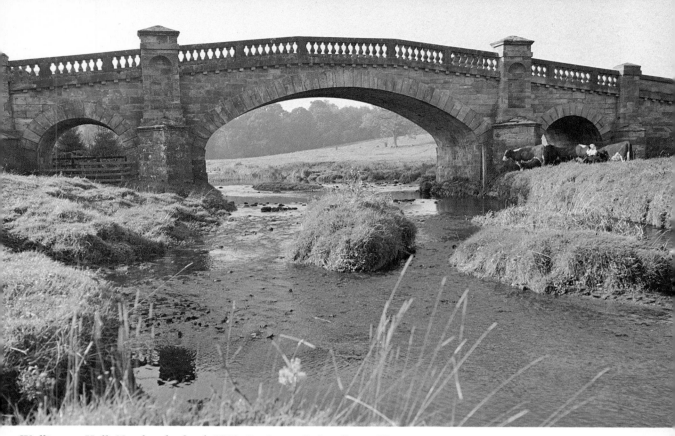

Wallington Hall, Northumberland. 1760. By James Paine. See p. 70.

Stourhead, Wilts. Over the lake. 1762. See p. 75.

Tickford Bridge, Newport Pagnell, Bucks. Over the Lovat. 1810. By Henry Provis. See p. 84.

Craigellachie Bridge, Grampian. Over the Spey. 1813. By Thomas Telford. See p. 88.

bridge. By Thomas Pritchard; the design probably finalized after Pritchard's death by the ironmaster Abraham Darby. One semi-circular cast-iron arch composed of five parallel ribs. 100-foot span. Side arches were inserted in the stone abutments in 1821 in place of the wooden ones that had been erected around 1800 to lighten the abutments which were showing signs of subsiding towards the river.

Yorkshire, North

Scarborough Spa Bridge near the Grand Hotel (originally a carriage drive; now restricted to pedestrians) 1827. By a little-known engineer, presumably a local man, called Outhett. Four cast-iron arches with ribs supporting the roadway, each of 66-foot span. Light iron railing. Stone piers.

WALES

Gwent

Chepstow over the Wye 1815 (strengthened 1889). Replaced a wooden bridge erected in 1647 in place of an earlier one destroyed in the Civil War. By Rennie. Five cast-iron arches resting on rounded stone piers. Iron railing with ornamental panel over the centre of each arch.

Gwynedd

Betws-y-coed Waterloo Bridge over the Conway. 1815 (strengthened 1923). By Telford. Cast iron between stone abutments. Wrought-iron railings. One 150-foot span. An inscription in cast iron occupying the whole length of the arch-ring reads, 'Constructed in the same year the battle of Waterloo was fought,' and the open-work spandrels are filled by cast-iron representations of the rose, thistle, shamrock and leek. The iron came from the foundry of William Hazledine, the Shropshire ironfounder.

Abermule over the Severn north-east of Newtown 1852. Replaced a bridge destroyed by floods. Cast and wrought iron. One flattish arch of 109-foot span. Stone abutments. A cast-iron inscription in the arch-ring reads, 'This second iron bridge in the county of Montgomery was erected in 1852.'

Chepstow, Gwent. Over the Wye. 1815. By John Rennie.

West Glamorgan

Clydach over the Tawe   1824. Single cast-iron arch of four ribs reinforced with Gothic-style braces. Almost the sole remnant of an eighteenth-century ironworks, now defunct.

SCOTLAND

Grampian

Craigellachie over the Spey   1813 (restored 1963). By Thomas Telford. Cast iron. One segmental arch of 150-foot span. Latticed arch ribs. Spandrels strengthened with lattices of narrow bars. Stone abutments surmounted by round castellated towers. The iron came from Hazledine's foundry. The bridge is no longer in use.

5

Canal Bridges and Aqueducts

If iron and the new uses to which it was put were among the keys that opened the way to the Industrial Revolution, another key material was coal, used to smelt iron, to raise steam and eventually to drive railway locomotives. A problem was to get the coal, of which Britain had plenty underground, from the places where it was mined to the places where it was needed. Water transport was the obvious answer for so heavy and bulky a commodity, since heavy goods had been carried by water since the Middle Ages, as described in Chapter 2, either down the navigable stretches of rivers or from port to port along the coast. The idea of building artificial waterways for the transport of coal was conceived by the third Duke of Bridgewater and implemented by the engineer he employed, James Brindley (1716–72). Brindley, along with Smeaton who was eight years older, may be regarded as the first of the remarkable line of civil engineers referred to in Chapter 2 as being central to the achievements of the Industrial Revolution. He has not been mentioned before because his energies were largely taken up with the design of canals, of the bridges over them and of the aqueducts that carried them.

His Bridgewater Canal, opened in 1761, was the first in Britain. It started inside the Duke's coal-mines at Worsley and carried coal for ten miles to the growing industrial city of Manchester, avoiding the navigationally difficult Mersey and Irwell rivers. Its success created an enthusiasm for canal building which lasted until it was brought to an end by the succeeding enthusiasm for railways. After 1761 three thousand miles of canals were dug in the space of eighty years, mostly in the Midlands and north-western England, necessitating three hundred Acts of Parliament to license them. So obsessed was Brindley with the utility of canals that, in giving evidence before a House of Commons committee considering one of these Acts, he declared that the only usefulness of a river was 'to supply canals with water'.

Brindley and other celebrated engineers such as Telford and Rennie were commissioned to build canals in many other parts of Britain as industrialists and investors began to appreciate their potential. The prime mover, for example, in promoting Brindley's most important subsequent canal, the Grand Trunk (now known as the Trent and Mersey Canal) was Josiah Wedgwood; canals, it was obvious, would especially benefit the pottery industry because they would avoid the breakages suffered when its products were transported by pack-horse or horse-drawn wagon, and they could also convey the industry's raw materials. Canals were most economical for the conveyance of heavy cargoes, but before the railways they were used for many other goods, including cattle and even on occasions to carry troops. In his book on English canals Eric de Maré quotes the following from *The Times* of 19 December 1806: 'The first division of the troops that are to proceed by Paddington Canal to Liverpool, and thence by transports for Dublin, will leave Paddington today, and will be followed by others tomorrow and on Sunday. By this mode of conveyance the men will be only seven days in reaching Liverpool.' Brindley's Grand Trunk Canal was built in 1766-7. It was 140 miles long and required 109 road bridges and 106 aqueducts besides locks, tunnels and other works.

Telford's first major English canal was the Ellesmere Canal, which with its branches was 112 miles long. His last was the Birmingham and Liverpool Junction, now part of the Shropshire Union. It linked Brindley's Wolverhampton Canal with his own Ellesmere Canal and created a highly economic shortened route between Liverpool, Manchester and Birmingham. It was Britain's last important canal undertaking except for the Manchester Ship Canal, opened as late as 1894, which brought a temporary revival of canal traffic in spite of the competition of the railways.

Scotland's first canals, such as the Monkland Canal begun in 1770, were primarily, like the first English canals, for the transport of coal, but one important canal, the Forth and Clyde, begun two years earlier and designed by Smeaton, had the more general purpose of linking the eastern to the western Lowlands where industry was developing rapidly. In 1818 it was extended by Hugh Baird as far as Edinburgh. However, by far the most ambitious canal-building enterprise in Scotland – though not the most successful commercially – was the Caledonian Canal, begun by Telford in 1804 and linking up a number of lochs in order to create a waterway running diagonally right across the Highlands and thus enabling shipping to avoid the dangerous northern seas. The Scottish canal systems do not join the English at any point.

Telford's Highland canals involved numerous locks and other engineering works but, owing to the small number of roads in the area, relatively few bridges. The English canals, in contrast, since they had constantly to cross the country's complex network of country roads and farm tracks, had to be furnished with an enormous number of small bridges – small because canals were narrow compared with many of the rivers which the bridges described in the foregoing chapters had to cross. They were normally the work of the engineer who was in charge of building the canal, or one of his assistants. Professional architects were not involved as they were in the case of rivers, though men such as Telford and Rennie could perhaps claim to be both.

Canal bridges are of two kinds: what are called 'accommodation bridges' carrying roads or farm-tracks across canals, and 'roving bridges' needed when the tow-path moves from one bank of the canal to the other – towing by horses, it hardly needs saying, was the regular means of propelling barges when the canal system was built. Not until many years afterwards were barges equipped with engines. These two kinds of bridge are of similar construction – brick or stone arches with the arch usually quite steeply humped to give its short span enough rise to let barges pass underneath. The roving bridges are generally the more steeply humped of the two. An ingenious variation of the roving bridge can be seen in places on the Stratford-on-Avon and the Staffordshire and Worcestershire Canals. This is the 'split bridge' in which a pair of iron brackets takes the place of the usual arch, with a gap of no more than an inch left at their central meeting-point. The rope towing a barge can be slipped through this gap, which saves casting it off at the bridge and re-attaching it.

Aldersley Junction, West Midlands. Roving bridge over the Staffordshire and Worcestershire Canal. 1781.

Canal bridges are of course single arched, as the piers between arches would obstruct the traffic. The arch is of brick or stone according to the locality – brick mostly in the Midlands and stone in the North – with its outer ring often painted white to give the steersman, who has to guide a laden barge precisely through the centre, better visibility at night. There are also some iron bridges – mostly by Telford. The design of canal bridges is always unpretentious and they are generally satisfactorily moulded into their landscape of tow-paths and embankments with the aid of curving wing-walls and parapets. Occasional variations from the usual arched bridge are the swing bridge which opens to let the traffic through and – notably on the Oxford Canal and on the Welsh section of the Shropshire Union Canal – the drawbridge, operating like those over the moats of medieval castles. But by and large canal bridges show little variation. Only a few typical examples are therefore included in the list at the end of this chapter.

The canal-building age did, however, produce another and a far more spectacular type of bridge structure deserving greater consideration here: the aqueduct which, especially in mountainous regions such as North Wales, offered a unique challenge to the engineers and marks the heroic age of canal construction. Canals require level waterways, and chains of locks stepping up and down the hillsides are costly to build and slow the traffic passing through them. It was again the third Duke of Bridgewater who conceived the idea of leading a canal on a level path above a river-valley, allowing the river and its own traffic to flow unimpeded beneath it.

After making the Grand Tour as a young man of twenty-two, during which he no doubt saw some of the aqueducts by which the Romans provided their cities with a water-supply, and studying the Canal du Midi in France, at that time Europe's largest artificial waterway, the Duke inspired Brindley to incorporate an aqueduct in his Bridgewater Canal. This, the Barton Aqueduct, crossing the Irwell valley, was Britain's first navigable aqueduct. It was opened to traffic in 1761 and was built of brick with stone piers supporting three segmental arches, the middle one spanning 63 feet. It continued in use until 1893 when the river was supplanted by the Manchester Ship Canal and the Barton aqueduct by a movable one – see page 102.

When the Duke built a branch of his Bridgewater Canal connecting it to the estuary of the Mersey near Runcorn he planned for it to cross the river at Stretford on an aqueduct consisting of a single brick arch with stone spandrels spanning 66 feet. This was completed in 1765 and is still there although additional arches, to allow flood-water to flow away more quickly, were added in 1830.

Brindley built a number of other aqueducts, including one at Rugeley, Staffordshire, in 1769, which carries the Trent and Mersey Canal over the River Trent, and another, in 1771, at Great Haywood which carries the Staffordshire

Great Haywood Aqueduct, Staffs. On the Staffordshire and Worcestershire Canal. 1771. By James Brindley.

and Worcestershire Canal over the same river. Both are still in use. Brindley's aqueducts are of straightforward arch construction with the waterway along which the barges travel contained in rectangular stone troughs lined with puddled clay. Later designers added large buttresses to strengthen the piers and particularly to withstand the pressure of the water in the trough, thus giving their structures a more massive appearance. An example is the Kelvin Aqueduct at Glasgow, designed in 1787 by Robert Whitworth (1732–99), Brindley's chief assistant and afterwards the engineer for the Thames and Severn Canal (from 1782) and for the Forth and Clyde Canal (from 1785). His Kelvin Aqueduct had four arches of 50-foot span supported on huge triangular piers. At the time it was completed it was the largest aqueduct yet built in Britain.

John Rennie, following the architectural fashion of his time, added Classical embellishments to his aqueducts; for example the Dundas Aqueduct on the Kennet and Avon Canal at Limpley Stoke in Wiltshire, which, when it was completed in 1810, effectively linked London to Bristol by water. Another example is the Lune Aqueduct by Alexander Stevens (1730–96), carrying the Lancaster Canal (begun by Brindley and Whitworth and completed by Rennie) over the Lune. This aqueduct was unique in its time for having its upper stonework reinforced internally with iron bars.

After the great Severn floods of 1795, in which Telford's iron bridge at Buildwas, Shropshire (see Chapter 4) was swept away – it was however rebuilt and lasted until 1905 – Telford started to become involved with aqueducts and, most important, to experiment with designs using iron. In 1795 he designed the Longdon-on-Tern Aqueduct carrying his Shrewsbury Canal over the Tern. Here not only is the rectangular trough holding the water made of cast-iron plates, but the structure's three spans are supported on triple cast-iron piers. This aqueduct still stands but is no longer used. It was claimed by Telford to have been the first iron aqueduct, but this was disputed by another engineer Benjamin Outram (1764–1805), who claimed that his own iron aqueduct on the Derby Canal had been completed a month earlier. Such rivalry is an indication of the prestige that was attached to these late-eighteenth-century engineering achievements.

Having demonstrated the feasibility of iron for both the trough and its supports, Telford went on, also in 1795, to construct his masterpiece among aqueducts, the Pont-y-Cysyllte Aqueduct near Llangollen in North Wales, which Sir Walter Scott declared was the most impressive work of art he had ever seen and which at Telford's own request appears in the background of the official portrait of him, by Samuel Lane, painted in 1822 when he was elected president of the Institution of Civil Engineers. The Cysyllte Aqueduct (see also page 105) carries the Ellesmere Canal over the wide valley of the Dee in a cast-iron trough supported on iron arch-ribs which span between stone piers, nineteen in number and 120 feet high. Citizens in the 1790s were astonished by the sight of heavy barges sailing along so high up in the air. To such an extent has the British canal system now fallen into disuse – in contrast to continental systems where new canals continue to be built – that many Britons in the 1990s would be astonished by the same sight.

Not far away at Chirk, also on the Ellesmere Canal, is another aqueduct by Telford nearly as spectacular, in this case with stone arches and only the trough of iron. Pont-y-Cysyllte was in fact exceptional in having both the arches and the trough of iron, but on others of his canals Telford built many small bridges wholly of iron, notably along the Oxford Canal for which, when he widened part of it in 1829, he designed a standard prefabricated cast-iron bridge. This was a rationalization of bridge construction that railway engineers were soon to imitate and that was to re-emerge more than a century later when standard bridges in reinforced concrete were employed in the construction of the mid-twentieth-century motorways.

Pont-y-Cysyllte Aqueduct, near Llangollen, North Wales. Over the Dee valley. 1795. By Thomas Telford.

A Selection of Typical Canal Bridges, listed by Counties

ENGLAND

Cheshire

Bosley (between Macclesfield and Leek) over the Macclesfield Canal. 1829. Stone. Elliptical arch with keystone surmounted by a heavy string-course. Adjoins a flight of locks.

Gloucestershire

Wheatenhurst over the Gloucester and Berkeley Ship Canal Swing bridge. 1826. Wood; upper parts painted white.

Wheatenhurst, Glos. Swing bridge over the Gloucester and Berkeley Ship Canal. 1826.

Bosley, Cheshire. Over the Macclesfield Canal. 1829.

Greater London

Brentford over the Grand Union Canal between Brentford and Oster-ley Roving bridge. 1820. Cast iron between brick abutments. Inscribed 'Horseley Iron Works.'

London

Regent's Park Macclesfield Bridge over the Regent's Canal. 1815. By James Morgan, assistant to John Nash (1752–1835), who appointed him engineer to the Regent's Canal Company in 1812. Named after Lord Macclesfield who was chairman of the company when the canal was opened in 1820. Three segmental brick arches, one over the waterway and two land arches, supported on fluted cast-iron Greek Doric columns. Circular holes in the spandrels. Iron railings. The bridge was accidentally blown up in 1874 when a barge carrying gunpowder exploded while passing beneath it. It was repaired, but with the columns facing a different way so that the grooves worn by tow-ropes are now in unlikely positions.

97

Northamptonshire

Braunston where the Oxford Canal joins the Grand Union Pair of iron bridges linked by a small stone bridge and with stone abutments. 1829, the year when Telford straightened the northern stretch of Brindley's Oxford Canal of 1770–90 (Telford believed in the straightest practicable runs notwithstanding that these involved making cuttings and embankments, whereas Brindley's earlier canals wound about following the contours of the landscape). Probably by Telford, who designed a number of standardized canal bridges. These examples are made of large precast units. Lettered on arch-ring 'Horseley Iron Works'.

Stoke Bruerne over the Grand Union Canal (London to Hull) Accommodation bridge with round stone buttresses and brick parapets. Around 1800. Elliptical arch. In a canalside warehouse near by is housed the Museum of British Waterways.

Braunston, Northants. Over the Oxford Canal. 1829. By Thomas Telford.

Whitchurch, Shropshire. Drawbridge over the Union Canal.

Shropshire

Whitchurch over the Shropshire Union Canal   Wooden drawbridge, raised manually. Date unknown – the canal was begun in 1789 but a wooden bridge, if of this date, is likely to have been renewed since.

Staffordshire

Great Haywood where the Staffordshire and Worcestershire Canal joins the Trent and Mersey Canal   Roving bridge. Around 1770. Brick. Steeply humped with curving wing-walls. This and the roving bridge at Aldersley Junction (see below) are typical of many similar.

Tyrley over the Shropshire Union Canal   Accommodation bridge. Around 1790. Probably by Telford who built the canal. Stone. Dramatically tall and narrow elliptical archway over a deep ravine.

Dicks Lane Bridge, Warwicks. A split bridge on the Stratford-on-Avon Canal. Around 1812.

Warwickshire

Dicks Lane Bridge over the Stratford-on-Avon Canal   Split bridge with gap in centre for passing tow-rope (see page 91). Around 1812. Cast iron between vertical brick abutments.

West Midlands

Aldersley Junction over the Staffordshire and Worcestershire Canal near where it joins the Shropshire Union north-west of Wolverhampton   1781. Roving bridge in brick. Segmental main arch plus small semi-circular arch over the tow-path. Curved wing-walls.

Wiltshire

Wilcot   Ladies' Bridge over the Kennet and Avon Canal. 1808. By Rennie. One stone arch. An unexpectedly ornate example, enriched with vermiculated rustication, swags and medallions and a partly balustraded parapet.

A Selection of Canal Aqueducts, listed by Counties (by Regions in Scotland)

ENGLAND

Cheshire

Bollington carrying the Macclesfield Canal over a road 1829. By Thomas Brown, a Manchester engineer. Stone. One semi-circular arch with a subtle curve between it and the wing-walls.

Bollington, Cheshire. Aqueduct on the Macclesfield Canal. 1829. By Thomas Brown.

Barton Aqueduct on the Manchester Ship Canal. 1893. By Williams, Abernethy and Hunter. A movable aqueduct replacing the one by Brindley.

Derbyshire

Lea Wood near Cromford, carrying the Cromford Canal over the Derwent 1791. By William Jessop (1745–1814). One unusually large (80-foot span) stone arch.

Greater Manchester

Barton Movable aqueduct on the Manchester Ship Canal, replacing Brindley's aqueduct of 1761 (see page 92). 1893. By Williams, Abernethy and Hunter. An iron trough 235 feet long carried on twin steel girders pivoted on a central island. When open it allows traffic to pass along the ship canal and when closed to pass over the aqueduct.

Marple carrying the now-disused Peak Forest Canal over the Goyt 1794. By Benjamin Outram. Handsome stone aqueduct of three semi-circular arches, each of 60-foot span, with pilasters between, supported on tall cylindrical piers. The spandrels have circular holes like William Edwards's Welsh road bridges (see page 55).

Macclesfield Bridge, Regent's Park, London. 1815. By James Morgan. See p. 97.

Great Haywood, Staffs. Roving bridge where the Staffordshire and Worcestershire and the Trent and Mersey Canals join. Around 1770. See p. 99.

*Dundas Aqueduct, Limpley Stoke, Wilts. On the Kennet and Avon Canal. 1805. By John Rennie.
See p. 104.*

Kirkliston, Lothian. Aqueduct on the Union Canal. 1820. See p. 106.

Stretford carrying the Bridgewater Canal over the Mersey   1765. By Brindley. Brick. One segmental arch.

Lancashire

Garstang   Wyre Aqueduct carrying the Lancaster Canal over the Wyre. 1798. By Rennie. Stone. One elliptical arch.

Lune Aqueduct near Lancaster carrying the Lancaster Canal over the Lune   1793. By Alexander Stevens. Stone. Five semi-circular arches each of 50-foot span with dentilled cornice above them and parts of the parapet balustraded.

Shropshire

Longdon carrying the Shrewsbury Canal over the Tern   1795. By Telford (he claimed it was the first aqueduct in iron – see page 94). Rectangular trough

Lune Aqueduct near Lancaster. 1793. By Alexander Stevens.

Longdon Aqueduct, Shropshire. On the Shrewsbury Canal. 1795. By Thomas Telford.

of cast-iron plates supported on triple cast-iron piers, formed of a central vertical member flanked by sloping members beneath the walls of the trough. Three spans.

Staffordshire

Burton-upon-Trent carrying the Grand Trunk (Trent and Mersey) Canal over the Dove   1766. By Brindley (his largest surviving aqueduct). Twenty-three low arches. Stone with brick parapets.

Great Haywood carrying the Staffordshire and Worcestershire Canal over the Trent   1771. By Brindley. Brick and stone. Four segmental arches.

Rugeley carrying the Trent and Mersey Canal over the Trent   1796. By Brindley. Stone and brick. Six segmental arches.

Wiltshire

Limpley Stoke   Dundas Aqueduct carrying the Kennet and Avon Canal over the Avon. 1805. By Rennie. Stone. Three arches, the centre one, of 65-foot span, over the waterway segmental; the smaller side arches over the tow-path parabolic. Double pilasters between arches, single pilasters between side arches and outward-curving wing-walls. Full entablature above surmounted by balustraded parapets. The Avoncliff Aqueduct further along the same canal is another example of Rennie's more monumental style.

Yorkshire, West

Stanley Ferry near Wakefield carrying the Aire and Calder Navigation over the Calder 1836. By George Leather. Said to be the largest cast-iron aqueduct in the world. Trough 165 feet long suspended by wrought-iron hangers from a pair of cast-iron segmental arches.

WALES

Clwyd

Chirk carrying the Ellesmere Canal over the Ceiriog valley south-east of Llangollen (beyond Offa's Dyke) 1796. By Telford. Stone, with canal trough of cast iron. Ten high semi-circular arches each of 40-foot span. The canal runs 70 feet above the river level.

Pont-y-Cysyllte carrying the Ellesmere Canal over the Dee valley near Llangollen 1795. By Telford. Cast-iron canal trough supported on four iron arch-ribs each spanning 45 feet between nineteen tapering stone piers 120 feet high. The piers are solid for the first 70 feet; then hollow to reduce the weight. The pier immediately south of the river bears a commemorative inscription. The width of the waterway is 11 ft 10 ins including an iron tow-path 4 ft 8 ins wide carried on brackets over the water.

Powys

Berriew carrying the Montgomeryshire Canal over the Rhiw 1796 (repaired 1889). Two river and two land arches. By John and Thomas Dadford, two of the three engineer sons of Thomas Dadford who had been construction engineer under Brindley on the Staffordshire and Worcestershire Canal in 1768.

SCOTLAND

Lothian

Kirkliston carrying the Union Canal over the Almond valley 1820. Rock-faced stone. Five segmental arches with tall tapering piers between.

Strathclyde

Glasgow Kelvin Aqueduct carrying the Forth and Clyde Canal over the Kelvin. 1787. By Whitworth. Four round stone arches of 50-foot span between large triangular piers. These and the arches heavily rusticated.

Kelvin Aqueduct, Glasgow. On the Forth and Clyde Canal. 1787. By Robert Whitworth.

6

Railway Bridges and Viaducts

As each successive chapter of this book has demonstrated, the development of the design of bridges is inseparable from the development of transport. In the second decade of the nineteenth century a new form of transport was devised: the railway. It expanded energetically if sometimes too impetuously – when regarded as a financial investment – throughout the remainder of the century. Britain's road network, which now covered the whole country, was thereby duplicated by a second network of railway lines. Nearly all the rivers that the roads had needed bridges to get over had to be crossed by a second set of bridges to carry the railways, and in addition the railways themselves had to bridge a great many of the roads. This is to say nothing of the many small bridges – called cattle-creeps – that had to be built beneath embankments for the movement of livestock when a railway cut off one part of a farm from another. Even leaving cattle-creeps aside it has been estimated that over 25,000 railways bridges were constructed between 1830 and 1860, more than doubling the number of bridges already existing.

The design and construction of this formidable number of new bridges was an important part of the railway-building enterprise. It was in fact integral to it, since a bridge is but a continuation of the permanent way over a void. Bridge building therefore came into the hands of the railway engineers instead of those of the architects who by this time were responsible for the design of most important road bridges. Railway bridges in any case were necessarily an engineering task because they required scientific skill and the ability to improvise solutions to unprecedented technical problems – not only, in the early days, to invent the structures required but also the tools and techniques for putting them together – and only engineers possessed this ability.

It was an age when technological progress aroused interest far outside the engineering profession. The achievements of the Industrial Revolution, including the increased mobility the railways offered to everyone, evoked a sense of wonder among the population generally and a sense of participating in the creation of the whole new range of structures that could be seen arising all over the country, with the result, for example, that crowds lined the waterfront to watch the great iron tubes that Robert Stephenson (1803–59) had invented for his Britannia Bridge across the Menai Strait being lifted into place, and assembled in great numbers to see many similar operations. Men like Stephenson and Brunel achieved nation-wide celebrity.

Railway engineers had now and then some tricky situations to deal with, especially when building over rivers, and came up at times with perhaps over-ingenious solutions which nevertheless impressed the first railway historians like Frederick Williams. Here is an account of a bridge installed on the Shoreham–Chichester line when it was built in 1845, quoted from Williams's book *Our Iron Roads*, published in 1852:

There is a kind of bridge on the South Coast Railway which is worthy of notice. It is over the Arun, below Arundel, and is the first of its kind. At this point the Company was bound to leave a clear waterway of sixty feet for the passage of shipping, and this had to be accomplished by a contrivance called a telescope bridge. The rails, for a length of 144 feet, are laid upon a massive timber platform, strengthened with iron, and trussed by means of rods, extending from its extremities to the top of a strong framework of timber, rising 34 feet above the level of the roadway in the middle of the platform, the framework being ornamented so as to appear like an arch. Beneath this central framework and one-half of the platform are mounted 18 wheels, upon which the whole structure may be moved backwards and forwards, so as to be either clear of the river, or to project its unsupported half across it, to form a bridge for the passage of trains. To provide for moving this platform, when it is necessary to open the waterway, a second portion of the railway, 63 feet long, is laid upon a moveable platform, which may be pushed aside laterally, while the end of the larger platform is pushed longitudinally into its place. Two men and a boy are able to open this bridge in about five minutes, the operation being performed by toothed wheels and racks, wrought by winches.

This structure was superseded in 1862 by another movable bridge of a different design.

Fortunately the vast majority of railway bridges were of their nature simpler and more straightforward. The first of any kind – if it can be classed as a railway bridge – was built in 1727, long before the establishment of a passenger-carrying railway system. It was a stone arch carrying a wooden tramway from the Tanfield Moor colliery in County Durham over a stream. It is still there. The first railway line in the modern sense, the Stockton and Darlington Railway, was opened in 1825, constructed by George Stephenson

(1781–1848), and had a number of bridges. The first – and therefore the first true railway bridge in Britain – a three-arch stone bridge at Darlington over the Skerne (see list at the end of this chapter), still carries traffic. Also on a branch of the Stockton–Darlington line was the first skew bridge, built over the Gaunless in 1830 by Thomas Storey (1789–1859), a cousin of Stephenson and later the chief engineer of the Great North of England Railway. A skew bridge, a type increasingly used by railway engineers, is one which makes the crossing of a road or river at an oblique angle. It involves rather complicated setting out and cutting of the masonry or brickwork (in geometrical terms a skew arch has the form of an oblique slice through a semi-cylinder), but it has the advantage that the railway line need not change direction in order to approach the road or river at right-angles, thus avoiding unwanted curves. There is a good solid example in brick between Slough and Maidenhead on the main Great Western line.

The earliest railway engineers preferred arched bridges. These were of brick or stone (more commonly brick even in regions where buildings were of stone) and were often skew bridges for the reason just mentioned. However railways, being a typical product of the Industrial Revolution, were the scene of the interaction between means and ends referred to in earlier chapters: new techniques creating new possibilities and the desire to exploit these encouraging the improvement of techniques and the development of still newer ones. As railway building progressed therefore, new forms of bridge construction emerged, most notably the more scientific use of iron, the railway engineers being able to build on Telford's earlier experiments with iron road bridges. Railway bridges posed structural problems far more complex than did road bridges; for example the greater weight of a train, especially when measured in terms of the weight concentrated on one axle, compared with that of a horse-drawn carriage or wagon however heavily loaded, and the vibration caused by the nature of its locomotion and the speed of its passage.

The first iron railway bridge was one of George Stephenson's on the Stockton–Darlington line – at West Auckland. Built in 1825 it crossed the Gaunless stream and had five spans of 12 ft 5 ins each, all consisting of a pair of fish-shaped trusses formed out of round wrought-iron bars with baluster-like uprights supporting the wooden deck. It was replaced in 1901 but is preserved as an exhibit outside the National Railway Museum at York. A favourite subsequent technique was to use cast-iron arched ribs with the spandrels filled by a trellis of iron struts – again following Telford's example – which helped to support the whole length of the track. One such bridge still exists at Peterborough, carrying a railway line over the Nene. Robert Stephenson, the son of George Stephenson and the most eminent of the early railway engineers, built a number of similar iron-arch bridges on the London–Birmingham line, but they have all by now been replaced in concrete.

Timber, rather surprisingly, was used for some of the early railway bridges, including a form of laminated timber arch first devised by John Green (1787–1852) and his brother Benjamin (died 1858) and employed in their Ouseburn and Willington viaducts on the Newcastle and North Shields Railway, which was completed in 1839. Their arches were built up of fourteen layers of timber. Laminated timber construction was further developed by Charles Vignoles (1793–1875), notably on the North Western Railway between Skipton and Lancaster, and Isambard Kingdom Brunel (1806–59), who succeeded Robert Stephenson as the most famous of all railway engineers, built a laminated timber bridge over the Avon at Bath in 1840, but all the bridges constructed by this method have now been superseded. Brunel also built timber viaducts on the South Devon, Cornwall and West Cornwall railways in the 1850s, for example at Treviddo where the track was supported on fan-shaped timber trusses springing from stone piers, and at St Germans where the piers, too, were of timber. Several of these viaducts survived into the twentieth century. The last to survive, at College Wood between Penryn and Falmouth, was replaced by a steel viaduct in 1934.

The first time cast-iron girders were used for a really large bridge was when Robert Stephenson built his High Level Bridge at Newcastle-upon-Tyne in

High Level Bridge, Newcastle-upon-Tyne. 1845. By Robert Stephenson. In foreground, the swing bridge of 1876 (see Chapter 9), by John F. Ure.

1845. But this much-favoured material presented many problems resulting from the stresses placed on it by the passage of trains. The relative brittleness of cast iron has already been alluded to and there were several collapses, especially of girder bridges, including at least one of Robert Stephenson's. However a good many bridges of this material continued in use for several years. Eventually, after a cast-iron girder bridge at Norwood Junction on the Brighton line collapsed in 1891, an inspecting officer's report recommended the replacement of all cast-iron bridges by steel. The London, Brighton and South Coast Railway company did so forthwith and the other companies soon followed.

But this is to anticipate the introduction of steel late in the nineteenth century. Throughout the great age of railway building the usual material was iron, except for small bridges, which were just as often brick and stone, and except for the long viaducts which were nearly always arched structures, again of stone or brick. Though cast iron's brittleness in some circumstances caused difficulties, it proved satisfactory enough for the vertical piers of girder bridges since it is safe and strong under direct compression. A prominent example of a railway bridge supported on cast-iron piers was the Albert Edward Bridge carrying the Severn Valley line (now removed) over the Severn near Buildwas, Shropshire. It was built in 1863, was designed by John Fowler (1817–98) – who was made a baronet after he had been co-designer of the Forth Bridge (see p. 123) – and was supplied with iron by the Coalbrookdale foundry near by.

Around this time too, there was a fashion for exploiting the decorative potentialities of the casting process, and bridges were built with spandrels, panels and the like cast in the form of elaborate sculptural enrichments. An example can still be seen in the town of Derby. The arched railway bridge over Friargate, built for the Great Northern company in 1878, has decorative ironwork cast in the Derby foundry of Andrew Handyside. Blackfriars railway bridge over the Thames also has heraldic enrichments in cast iron.

Nevertheless the great engineers of the railway-building age employed wrought iron rather than cast iron for their most important bridges. Robert Stephenson used wrought-iron tension rods in combination with cast-iron girders in his High Level Bridge at Newcastle just referred to, and in his two tubular bridges, over the Menai Strait and the Conway River (both 1846), the tubes are wholly of wrought iron. Their construction, a long rectangular iron box inside which the trains ran as in a tunnel, was a somewhat primitive conception and was not widely adopted, its only virtue being that the trains were protected from the force of the wind when crossing a strait or estuary. A more advanced type of construction in wrought iron was employed by Brunel for the Royal Albert Bridge at Saltash on the Cornwall Railway, built in 1859. It followed the system used by him in an earlier bridge at Chepstow (1852) and had two main arches of wrought-iron tube combined with suspension chains

111

to counteract their outward thrust and ensure that the load on the supporting piers was directly vertical.

Complex systems like this were not however continued with, perhaps because in the meantime engineers had learnt more about stresses in beams and the lattice-girder type of bridge had therefore emerged. One of the first and finest examples of this type – in fact one of the most spectacular, and beautiful, railway bridges ever built – was the Crumlin Viaduct in South Wales, carrying the Taff Vale extension of the Newport, Abergavenny and Hereford Railway over the Ebbw Vale. It was designed in 1853, completed in 1857 and demolished as recently as 1967. Its engineers were Liddell and Gordon but the man mainly responsible was Thomas William Kennard (1825-93) from whose works at Falkirk, Scotland, the iron components for it were brought and who invented the type of lattice beam incorporated in it.

The Crumlin Viaduct was 1,500 feet long and 200 feet high and was wholly of iron, with eight spidery lattice piers supporting four lattice beams. Each pier was made up of fourteen hollow cast-iron columns grouped into a hexagonal formation and braced internally by horizontal 'distance girders' of cast iron and diagonal bars of wrought iron. The astonishingly narrow lattice beams were made up of parallel wrought-iron girders in the form of a triangulated truss.

The lattice-girder system was subsequently used for many railway bridges, including those across the Thames at Charing Cross (1864) and Blackfriars (also 1864), and the very long-span Runcorn Bridge, Cheshire – see the list at the end of this chapter. The ill-fated Tay Bridge near Dundee was also of lattice-girder construction. When this was built it was the longest iron bridge in the world. It was designed by Sir Thomas Bouch (1822-80), who was given his knighthood for doing so, and was completed in 1878. It collapsed during a gale the following year while a train was passing over it, plunging the whole train ninety feet down into the river and killing every one of the seventy-five people in it. The Board of Trade inquiry into the disaster reported that the bridge had been 'badly designed, badly constructed and badly maintained'.

The period of daring experiments in bridge construction now came to an end, for engineers were becoming more capable of exact mathematical calculation of stresses and the like. The next great railway bridge in fact, that over the Firth of Forth, begun in 1883 and completed in 1890 and designed by Sir Benjamin Baker (1840-1907) and Sir John Fowler, was designed, because of the Tay Bridge disaster, with an excessive margin of safety. It was built to withstand a wind-pressure of fifty-six pounds per square foot whereas thirty pounds is today regarded as sufficient – the Tay Bridge had been designed to withstand only twenty pounds.

The Forth Bridge follows a structural principle which at the time it was built was new to England but had been employed on a smaller scale in Germany since the 1860s by the engineer Heinrich Gerber. It is composed of three towers each supporting cantilevered arms balancing each other on either side of the tower and linked by short trussed spans. The bridge is approached from each shore by a lattice-girder viaduct on tall granite piers. It was the largest bridge of its kind in existence and remained so until the Quebec Bridge in Canada was completed in 1917 (after collapsing during construction in 1907). The giant size of the Forth Bridge makes it wonderfully impressive both when viewed across the water and to travel over. Nevertheless, employing such a variety of structural forms, it has not the clarity and elegance of, for example, the great road suspension bridges. It was not universally admired even at the time of its triumphant completion. William Morris wrote, 'There never would be an architecture in iron, every improvement in machinery being uglier and uglier until they reached the supremest specimen of all ugliness, the Forth bridge.'

The significance of the Forth Bridge was not its vast size or even its cantilever construction but the fact that the great tubes out of which its towers and cantilevers were built up were of steel. It was the first bridge to be made of mild steel rather than of iron. Steel, which came into structural use after Bessemer had invented his converter in 1856, is harder and more reliable than iron; moreover the stresses set up in it, and therefore the size of the beams, tubes etc. required, can be more precisely calculated. A defect of steel is that it rusts more readily than iron and has to be painted; hence the well-known interminable process of painting the exposed steel surfaces of the Forth Bridge, which add up to 145 acres.

Another impressive cantilever bridge followed in 1901, also in Scotland: the Connel Ferry Bridge. It carries a branch of the Caledonian Railway over Loch Etive in Strathclyde and was designed by Sir John Wolfe Barry (1836–1918), the engineer fifteen years earlier of London's Tower Bridge – see Chapter 9. The Connel Ferry Bridge has its cantilever girders hung from the tops of large raking struts. It, too, is of steel; in fact steel from the 1890s onwards became the usual material for the construction of railway bridges. In the case of bridges of moderate span, such as those over country roads, it was used for the most part in the simplest possible form: parallel girders with sides of bolted steel plates – serviceable but with little variety or special aesthetic interest.

In this century steel has been partly superseded as a structural material by reinforced concrete. By the time this occurred the age of railway building had long ended, but there exist a good number of concrete railway bridges built either as replacements or over newly built roads, and concrete – not reinforced – was used as far back as 1898 for a series of arch bridges on the Mallaig extension of the West Highland Railway, including the Glenfinnan Viaduct (see page 131). When the Adam Viaduct, near Wigan, was built in 1947 to replace an early viaduct of timber, the newest technical improvement, prestressed concrete, was used, but while on most of the new motorways the road bridges are of reinforced concrete, generally prestressed, the railway engineers have still preferred to build bridges of the conventional steel girder type, the principal recent refinement being the use of welding instead of riveting.

The next category of bridges we must deal with is railway viaducts, which have so far been described only in connection with the now demolished Crumlin Viaduct, built of iron. Most viaducts are of stone or brick arch construction, although sometimes they have been built of iron or steel lattice girders supported on stone piers, for example on the West Highland Railway and in South Wales, and there is a major viaduct of this type between Runcorn and Widnes over the Mersey.

As Britain's railway system grew a great many viaducts were required because of the need for the permanent way to be as level as possible, avoiding steep gradients. This was achieved across undulating country by excavating cuttings and raising embankments, but when the railway came to a broad valley it needed a viaduct to carry it across on an unvarying level just as the earlier canal system had needed aqueducts. Railway viaducts are therefore most frequent in hilly country, for example on the line from Settle to Carlisle built in 1870-8 as part of the Midland Railway. This line, a notable feat of engineering, but at the time of writing threatened with closure, has twenty large viaducts in its seventy-two-mile length, including some of the most splendid in Britain such as the Ribblehead Viaduct (see page 131). But viaducts are to be found in flatter country as well, carrying the railway over river valleys; also over the low-lying parts of towns as at Folkestone, Brighton and Stockport and over the southern suburbs of London. Some of the latter are of extraordinary length; the Bermondsey-Deptford viaduct has eight hundred and seventy-eight brick arches and is three and a half miles long. It constituted almost the whole of the first railway line to enter London - the London Bridge to Greenwich line, approved by Parliament in 1833 and carrying its first passengers in 1836.

Viaducts had many advantages when the railways penetrated into towns. They enabled stations to be placed more centrally, they needed little land and they avoided the need for level-crossings and for the railways to interfere with the existing street pattern. Building viaducts over towns sometimes however had the effect of lowering land and property values - or it was feared that it might do so. A proposal in the 1860s to build a viaduct in Glasgow was so strongly objected to on these grounds that the project was abandoned and the stations to which it was to have led had to be approached, north of the Clyde, by far more expensive tunnels.

Viaducts are among the most dramatic and, in relation to the landscape, the most pleasing, of all railway structures and added greatly to the excitements of railway travel for the early passengers. The first of the familiar type of arched viaduct (which of course had a prototype in the canal aqueduct - see Chapter

4) was built near Newton-le-Willows, Merseyside, over the Sankey Brook, at a place afterwards named Earlestown after Sir Hardman Earle, a North of England railway magnate. The viaduct was designed by George Stephenson in 1828 as part of his pioneering Liverpool–Manchester railway and had nine brick and stone arches on square piers 70 feet high. On a trial run over the line in August 1830, a month before it was formally opened by the Duke of Wellington, Stephenson himself drove the *Northumbrian*, the newest locomotive, with the actress Fanny Kemble with him on the footplate. Of the sensation of crossing the Sankey Viaduct she wrote afterwards: 'I stood up, and with my bonnet off drank the air before me. The wind, which was strong, or perhaps the force of our own thrusting against it, absolutely weighed my eyelids down. When I closed my eyes this sensation of flying was quite delightful, and strange beyond description; yet strange as it was, I had a perfect sense of security and not the slightest fear.' The second-class passengers on the earliest railway trains, riding as they did in open carriages, must have been similarly windswept.

There is one further category of railway bridge, contrasting in scale with the viaduct, that still has to be described: the footbridge by which passengers are instructed to cross the line at stations. For some reason station footbridges have been less fully recorded than other kinds of railway bridge although many are quite elegantly designed. They have not however such a long history because in the early days of railways it was not forbidden to step over the lines at the end of the platform. Most footbridges were therefore additions to stations already built. Their construction became general in the 1860s following Board of Trade inquiries into accidents that occurred as the speed and frequency of trains increased. In the 1870s the Board of Trade made it compulsory for all new stations to have either bridges or subways by which passengers could cross the line safely. This requirement did not apply to existing stations and many continued without either, as some small country stations do to this day.

Before footbridges became general there were overbridges forming part of the complex of station buildings. What is believed to have been the earliest example was built in 1841 at Normanton, West Yorkshire, the meeting-point of the York and North Midland, the North Midland and the Manchester and Leeds Railways. The station here was in a cutting and George Townsend Andrews (1805–55), a York architect, designed an overbridge on which the station offices were also carried and which led directly into a hotel. His design was later amended to place the offices alongside the platform but it still included a roofed footbridge leading into the hotel. Other footbridges forming part of the architecture of the station are at Nuneaton, Warwickshire, and at Lancaster. There the bridges are double with separate covered ways for passengers and luggage.

Taplow, Bucks. Station footbridge. 1884.

Most of the major railway companies had their own designs for footbridges, some of their standard designs being also adaptable for carrying footpaths over the line and for line-side use by railway maintenance staff; they had then to be built three feet higher than station footbridges since they did not start from platform level. The designs, of which some typical examples are listed at the end of this chapter (though their dates are in most cases difficult to determine) were normally the work of the companies' own engineers, sometimes in conjunction with an ironworks contractor, or of one of the engineer's architectural assistants, except when the footbridges formed part of new stations. Then they were designed by the architect or engineer responsible, who might or might not have been a member of the company's regular staff.

The first station footbridges were of wood or cast iron – there is a surviving wooden footbridge at Darlington North Road station – and thereafter, as in the case of other railway bridges, successively of wrought iron, steel and concrete as these materials in turn superseded the earlier ones. In most iron or steel bridges the parapets were also the main girders. Stairs were generally of wood on steel stringers. There is a spectacular open lattice example, supported on circular cast-iron columns, just north-west of Rugby. Footbridges were generally unroofed except when they were an integral part of the station

116

buildings. Then they were frequently provided with the additional comfort of glazed windows. When roofs were added they were most often of corrugated iron. Early footbridges of the cast-iron lattice-girder type with wooden flooring can still be seen on the old Great Northern and Midland lines. The North Eastern employed a particularly graceful arched lattice design, as did the Midland and various Scottish lines. The London and South Western used flanged steel-plate girders to replace their first wooden footbridges. The group of lines that merged to become the Southern Railway replaced many of their footbridges with a standard precast concrete pattern around 1930.

The valance of shaped vertical boards that provides a decorative edging to many station platform verandahs is also to be seen on footbridges, notably on the Great Western line where Taplow station has an exceptionally elegant and well-preserved example. In some places, for example Tilehurst, Berkshire, and Wootton Basset, Wiltshire (page 137), the stairs have nicely turned cast-iron balusters.

A Selection of Notable Railway Bridges, listed by Counties (by Regions in Scotland)

ENGLAND

Berkshire

Maidenhead over the Thames   1837 (widened 1892). By Brunel. Red engineering brick with stone trimmings. Two long elliptical arches each of 128-foot span with small round land arches over the tow-path. Paired pilasters between the arches, which have no less than ten courses of voissoirs. They are thought to have been the longest brick arches and those with the flattest curve yet built. Total length 760 feet. This is generally reputed to be the bridge shown in Turner's celebrated painting *Rain, Steam and Speed* and is designated as such by Pevsner in the Berkshire volume of his *Buildings of England*, but the bridge in the painting is more probably the Wharncliffe Viaduct at Hanwell (see page 127). Mr Michael Robbins, writing to the author, states the case for the latter as follows: 'It is a *dawn* scene – yellow not pink tones – and the train with the lighted headlamp on the engine must be travelling eastwards towards London. The road bridge on the left must therefore be on the south side of the railway line. The bridge over the Brent on the Uxbridge Road at Hanwell fits this; the Maidenhead one doesn't. The bridge or viaduct over which the train

Maidenhead Railway Bridge, Berks. Over the Thames. 1837. By I. K. Brunel.

is travelling is high, with rounded arches resting on tall piers. This fits Hanwell, but Maidenhead was and is the flattest brick arch possible.' He justly adds that Turner, like other artists, often rearranged elements in a landscape to produce precisely the composition he wanted so that one cannot look at his paintings for accurate topographical truth. A delightful account of a railway journey on the Great Western line into Paddington in Turner's company on a stormy summer day of the same year (1843) in which the picture was painted is given in a letter to John Ruskin from Mrs John Simon, quoted in the Dilecta section at the end of Ruskin's *Praeterita*.

Cheshire

Runcorn over the Mersey for the London and North Western Railway   1868. By William Baker (1817–78). Three wrought-iron lattice girders 75 feet above the river supported on stone piers. Arched stone portals at either end with castellated turrets. Approached at the Widnes end by a 59-arch brick viaduct. Baker was chief engineer of the London and North Western Railway for whom he designed several important stations.

118

Cornwall

Saltash Royal Albert Bridge over the Tamar (eastern approaches in Devon). 1859. By Brunel. Two main 455-foot spans plus smaller approach spans. Main spans have elliptical iron tubes 9 feet high acting as arches, with bar chains to counteract some of the thrust – an unusual construction. Pairs of rectangular stone piers support the approach viaduct and wider single piers the main spans, at either end of which the track passes through a stone archway which also supports the ends of the tubes. The bridge incorporates some of the ironwork Brunel had prepared for use on the Clifton suspension bridge (see page 143) when work on this was halted for lack of money.

Royal Albert Bridge, Saltash, Cornwall. Over the Tamar. 1859. By I. K. Brunel.

Kew Railway Bridge, Greater London. Over the Thames. 1868. By W. R. Galbraith.

Durham

Darlington   Carrying the first of all railway lines, the Stockton and Darlington, over the Skerne. 1825 (subsequently widened on the north side). Said to be by Ignatius Bonomi (1787–1870), but it is more probable that a design by the line's engineer George Stephenson was submitted for an opinion to, and received the approval of, Bonomi, a well-known architect who in 1819 had designed a bridge over the Wear at Lambton Castle not far away. This was altered afterwards and has now been demolished. The Skerne Bridge, of stone, has a stilted segmental arch, narrow land arches and curved wing-walls.

Tanfield Moor over the Causey Burn, carrying a wooden colliery tramway built to link Tanfield Moor Colliery with an earlier tramway   1727 – and therefore far earlier than any passenger-carrying railway. By Ralph Wood, a local mason. One elliptical stone arch of 105-foot span. Nicholas Hawksmoor wrote of it in 1736: 'a bold Arch lately built near Newcastle for the convenience of the Coal trade, which must be here mentioned for the largeness of its span'.

Greater London

Dulwich (Croxted Road)   1869. Ornamental cast-iron bridge carrying the Tulse Hill branch of the London, Chatham and Dover Railway. Main 22-foot span over the roadway; smaller arched spans over the footways. Cast-iron columns. Highly decorated iron railings. The initials AC in the spandrels of the arches stand for Alleyn's College.

Kew Railway Bridge over the Thames   1868. By W.R. Galbraith (1829–1914). Lattice-girder bridge of five spans with cylindrical cast-iron piers rising above the girders and highly ornamented. Brick abutments.

Shropshire

Buildwas   Albert Edward Bridge carrying the Severn Valley line over the Severn. 1862. By John Fowler. A comparatively late use of cast iron (from the neighbouring Coalbrookdale foundry). One segmental arch of multiple girders with vertical bracing in the spandrels.

Surrey

Chertsey   Lyne Bridge, a very late railway bridge required to carry the line from Chertsey to Virginia Water over the M25 motorway. 1980. By J.B. Manson, a British Rail engineer. A cable-stayed bridge with monolithic deck in prestressed concrete – believed to be the first cable-stayed railway bridge in the world. Two spans of 180 feet each. The two pylons, supporting the twin stay-cables and attached to the upper edge-beams of the deck, are 72 feet high.

Tyne and Wear

Newcastle-upon-Tyne

HIGH LEVEL BRIDGE over the Tyne   1845. By Robert Stephenson, advised by the Newcastle architect John Dobson (1787–1865). The first large bridge using wrought as well as cast iron. Six 125-foot spans each composed of four cast-iron arch ribs with the railway deck supported on cast-iron columns. Stone piers pierced with arches and a stone approach viaduct. A roadway beneath the railway track is suspended from the arches on wrought-iron rods. The High Level Bridge was a remarkable achievement in its day. 'The multiplicity of column-ribs, transverse and vertical braces', wrote Frederick Williams, in *Our Iron Roads* (1852, already quoted), 'produces a combination of beautiful lines seldom seen.'

KING EDWARD VII BRIDGE   The last great railway bridge, built some years after the end of the railway era and designed to supplement Stephenson's High

Level Bridge of sixty years before. 1905. By C.A. Harrison (1848–1916), chief engineer of the North Eastern Railway. Four spans of 40 feet, 300 feet, 300 feet and 190 feet, each consisting of five parallel steel lattice-girders 27 feet deep, set 11 feet apart. Piers of Norwegian granite. Tracks 112 feet above high water. Total length 1,150 feet.

Warwickshire

Stratford-upon-Avon (just south of Clopton Bridge, between it and the Shakespeare Memorial Theatre – see Chapter 1) 1823. By John Urpeth Rastrick (1780–1856) who was later the engineer in charge of the London–Brighton line, working in partnership with the ironfounder and locomotive builder Hazledine of Bridgnorth. Nine-arch brick bridge built to carry a horse-tramway from the town's wharf to Shipston-on-Stour; another bridge (see Tanfield Moor, Co. Durham) that is strictly pre-railway though only by a couple of years. It is now a public footbridge.

Yorkshire, North

Helwith over the Ribble, north of Settle on the line to Appleby and Carlisle 1870. By John Crossley (1812–79), chief engineer of the Midland Railway. Stone. Four low segmental arches with triangular cutwaters continued upwards to parapet level.

WALES

Gwynedd

Britannia Tubular Bridge over the Menai Strait, a mile to the west of Telford's great suspension bridge – see the next chapter 1846. By Robert Stephenson, with the architect Francis Thompson (ff. 1835) who designed many of the stations on the Chester-Holyhead line. Twin wrought-iron beams each consisting of a rectangular tube inside which the trains run. Four spans of 230 feet, 460 feet, 460 feet and 230 feet, the pier between the two main spans standing on the Britannia Rock. Rough-surfaced Anglesey stone towers 230 feet high, the tops of which, of dressed stone, are given a slightly Egyptian character. They were designed to support auxiliary chains but the tubes proved so strong that these were never added. The tubes were severely damaged by fire in 1970 and in order that rail traffic could be resumed as soon as possible it was decided not to reconstruct them but to replace them by segmental steel arches spanning between the original stone towers. This has radically altered the appearance of the bridge and compromised its straightforward character. At the same time a roadway was incorporated in it to relieve Telford's suspension bridge of the traffic on the A5 to Holyhead.

Conway, alongside Telford's suspension road bridge   1846. By Robert Stephenson. Tubular bridge similar in design and construction to his Britannia Bridge – see above. Two 400-foot spans between fortress-style stone abutments with machicolations.

SCOTLAND

Grampian

Spey Bridge near Grantown-on-Spey   1857. By Joseph Mitchell (1803–83), a pupil of Telford's who worked on most of the Highland railways. Iron beam with plated sides spanning between stone piers. Approached by a short viaduct of stone arches.

Lothian

Forth Bridge over the Firth of Forth west of Edinburgh   1883. By Sir John Fowler and Sir Benjamin Baker. Three tapered steel towers composed of tubular members, each with cantilevered arms balancing one another and linked across the centre of each 1,700-foot span by steel arch trusses of 680-foot span. The towers rest on small circular stone piers just above water level. The bridge is approached over a lattice-beam viaduct supported on tall stone piers, the whole structure with its approaches being a mile and a half long. The twin railway tracks, 150 feet above water level, are flanked by footways.

Strathclyde

Connel Ferry Bridge carrying the Ballachulish branch of the Callender and Oban Railway over the entrance to Loch Etive   The second largest cantilever

Connel Ferry Bridge, Loch Etive, Strathclyde. 1901. By Sir John Wolfe Barry.

bridge in Britain, after the Forth Bridge; also carries a toll road. 1901. By Sir John Wolfe Barry. Steel, on low granite piers. Main span 524 feet. Length of steel portion, 735 feet. Stone approach viaduct of varying spans. Total length with approaches, 1,020 feet.

A Selection of Railway Viaducts, listed by Counties (by Regions in Scotland)

ENGLAND

Cheshire

Congleton Viaduct over the Dane for the North Staffordshire line   1849. By G.W. Buck (1789–1854). Brick. Ten arches of 50-foot span.

Cornwall

Luxulyan 1839. Viaduct built to carry the railway, now closed, from Treffry granite quarries; also serves as an aqueduct. Eight stone arches 100 feet high.

Moorswater Viaduct west of Liskeard on the main Great Western line 1881. By R.P. Brereton (died 1894), Brunel's understudy. Stone. Eight semi-circular arches very thin at the crown. From it can be seen the remains of the pillars that carried Brunel's earlier timber viaduct – see page 110.

Cumbria

Smardale over the Scandal Beck and the now disused railway line from Kirkby Stephen to Tebay on the Settle-Carlisle line 1870. By John Crossley. Local limestone. Twelve arches 130 feet high. Length 710 feet. The highest viaduct on this line.

Derbyshire

Monsal Dale, near Bakewell on the line between Manchester and Ambergate originally engineered by George Stephenson 1860. Six stone arches. This was the viaduct reviled by John Ruskin when he wrote: 'Now every fool in Buxton can be in Bakewell in half an hour, and every fool in Bakewell at Buxton; which you think a lucrative process of exchange – you Fools Everywhere.'

Devonshire

Meldon Viaduct south-west of Okehampton on the Devon and Cornwall Railway 1871 (widened to take a second track 1879). By William Jacomb (1832–87). An all-iron lattice viaduct of the same type as the somewhat larger – and now demolished – Crumlin Viaduct in South Wales (see page 112), but built on a curve. It has similar lattice beams but its openwork piers, splayed out towards the base, are of wrought iron instead of cast iron. Six 90-foot spans. Track 150 feet above the ground. This railway line was closed to passenger traffic in 1968 but trains carrying ballast from Meldon quarry continue to cross the viaduct.

Meldon Viaduct, near Okehampton, Devon. 1871. By William Jacomb.

Durham

Hownes Gill Viaduct near Consett for the Stockton and Darlington Railway 1855. By Thomas Bouch. Firebrick. Eight arches on slender piers themselves pierced with narrow arches. Single track, now disused, 150 feet above the valley floor.

Essex

Chapple Viaduct over the Colne Valley near Wakes Colne 1847. By Peter Schuyler Bruff (1812–1900), engineer to the Eastern Union Railway. Light coloured local brick. Thirty-two semi-circular arches of 30-foot span. Arched opening in each pier. Total length 1,136 feet.

Greater London

Hanwell   Wharncliffe Viaduct over the Brent. 1838 (widened 1877). By Brunel. The first major engineering structure on his Great Western line. Yellow London stock brick with stone capitals to the slightly tapering piers. Elliptical arches. Eight 70-foot spans. 900 feet long. Track 65 feet above the ground. Over one of the piers, on the south side, are the arms of Lord Wharncliffe, who was chairman in 1835 of the Lords committee on the incorporating Bill. The directors of the Great Western Railway named the viaduct after him in gratitude. For the viaduct's association with Turner see under Maidenhead Bridge, Berkshire, above.

Wharncliffe Viaduct, Hanwell, Greater London. 1838. By I.K. Brunel.

Stockport Viaduct, Greater Manchester. 1839. By G.W. Buck.

Greater Manchester

Stockport over the roofs of the town   1839. By G.W. Buck. Twenty-seven arches 110 feet high. Total length 1,800 feet.

Wigan   Adam Viaduct. 1946. Of interest only because it was the first pre-stressed concrete railway bridge in Britain – precast on the Freyssinet system.

Hertfordshire

Digswell between Welwyn and Welwyn Garden City   1850. By Sir William Cubitt (1785–1861), consulting engineer for the Great Northern Railway. Brick. Forty arches 89 feet high.

Kent

Folkestone over the Foord Valley.   1843. By Sir William Cubitt. Brick. Nineteen arches nearly 100 feet high on slender piers only 6 feet wide at the top, tapering on all four sides.

London

Brixton carrying the London, Chatham and Dover Railway over the inner suburb of that name   1863. Brick arches. Typical of many railway viaducts leading over the south London suburbs to the terminal stations. It is crossed by a high-level iron lattice bridge of 1867.

Merseyside

Earlestown   Sankey Viaduct over the Sankey Brook, the first large railway viaduct (see page 115). 1828. By George Stephenson. Brick faced with stone. Nine semi-circular arches of 50-foot span on piers with splayed bases. 70 feet high.

Northamptonshire

Harringworth   Welland Viaduct over the river of that name. 1876. By John Underwood (1849-93), superintendent engineer of the Midland Railway. Blue and red brick. Eighty-two segmental arches on tall piers.

Northumberland

Berwick-on-Tweed   Royal Border Bridge over the Tweed. 1847. By Robert Stephenson. Stone piers. Twenty-eight brick arches 126 feet high and of 61-foot span. Total length 2,160 feet. Built on a slight curve.

Sussex, East

Brighton   London Road Viaduct over the town's northern suburbs. 1841. By J.U. Rastrick and David Mocatta (1806–82), a pupil of Sir John Soane and the architect of some elegant stations on the Brighton line. Thirty-seven arches. Built on a curve.

Sussex, West

Balcombe Viaduct over the Ouse, on the London–Brighton line north of Haywards Heath   1839. By Rastrick and Mocatta. Brick with stone dressings.

Royal Border Bridge, Berwick-on-Tweed. 1847. By Robert Stephenson.

Balcombe Viaduct, West Sussex. 1839. By Rastrick and Mocatta.

Thirty-seven semi-circular arches of 30-foot span. Openings in the piers. Balustraded parapets with small Italianate pavilions at each end. Track 92 feet above the ground. Length 1,437 feet. The tracks were recently welded to reduce vibration and safeguard the structure.

Tyne and Wear

Willington Viaduct for the Newcastle and North Shields Railway   1837. By John and Benjamin Green. Originally with arches of laminated timber (see page 110) which were replaced by iron in 1869. Seven arches of varying spans, the widest 128 feet. Stone piers.

Yorkshire, North

Knaresborough over the Nidd   1850. By Thomas Grainger (1794–1852). Stone. Castellated in an attempt to harmonize with the church and castle picturesquely sited on the river bank. Four semi-circular arches of 57-foot span, 78 feet high on stepped piers.

Ribblehead Viaduct near Chapel-le-Dale on the Settle–Carlisle line   1869. By John Crossley. Twenty-four arches of the local limestone, each of 45-foot span and 156 feet high, making it probably the tallest viaduct in Britain. Every sixth pier is made thicker than the others, so that if one collapsed only five more would do the same. Total length 1,328 feet.

SCOTLAND

Highland

Glenfinnan Viaduct over the Finnan at the northern end of Loch Shiel, on the extension to Mallaig of the West Highland Railway   1897. By Simpson and Wilson. The first concrete viaduct. Twenty-one arches of 50-foot span, 90 feet high. Wholly of mass concrete – perhaps the boldest use of this material since Roman times.

Lothian

Kirkliston   Viaduct built to carry the Edinburgh and Glasgow Railway over the Almond Valley. 1842. By Grainger. Stone. Thirty-two rock-faced arches. Dressed stone parapet.

Strathclyde

Ballochmyle Viaduct over the Ayr near Cumnock, for the Glasgow and South Western Railway 1846. By John Miller (1805–83). Red sandstone. Central span of 181 feet which, when the viaduct was completed and for fifty years afterwards, was the widest stone railway arch in the world. Six side arches of 50-foot span. Track 164 feet above the water.

Tayside

Dundee Tay Bridge, replacing the bridge destroyed in the famous disaster of 1879 – see page 112. 1885. By W.H. Barlow (1811–1902) and Sir Benjamin Baker. Wrought-iron lattice beams on brick arches. Eighty-five spans (seventy-four over the water), the largest 245 feet. 10,711 feet long and there-

Glenfinnan Viaduct, Highland. 1897. By Simpson and Wilson.

Tay Bridge, Dundee, Tayside. 1885. By W.H. Barlow and Sir Benjamin Baker.

fore the longest railway bridge in Britain. Track 83 feet above water level. Barlow helped to complete the Clifton suspension bridge (see page 143) and was consulted by Paxton over the calculation of the strength of the columns and girders of the 1851 Crystal Palace.

A Selection of Typical Railway Footbridges, listed by Counties

ENGLAND

Berkshire

Newbury Racecourse Prominent example of a long unroofed lattice steel station footbridge continuing over several platforms. The footbridge at New-bury's main station is a good example of the totally enclosed type, with steel girders supporting a wooden superstructure. Stairs of brick with continuous windows above.

133

Tilehurst 1892, when the station was rebuilt. Plate-sided bridge with wood valance to roof and wood-enclosed stairs with decorative cast-iron balusters.

Buckinghamshire

Taplow Iron lattice station footbridge supported on bracketed cast-iron columns painted black with G.W.R. monograms and other ornaments picked out in yellow. Corrugated iron roof. Decorative wood valances and wood staircase enclosures with finials on the gables, painted cream. One of the most attractive of all station footbridges.

Cumbria

Carlisle Citadel Long-span arched iron lattice station footbridge. A good example of this characteristic North British and Midland type.

Derbyshire

Charlesworth near Glossop over a single track (not at a station) Iron lattice construction – stairs as well as bridge – slightly arched on slender braced supports. Raised bolts on the lattice intersections create a decorative effect.

Charlesworth, near Glossop, Derbyshire. Footbridge.

Tanfield Moor, Co. Durham. Carrying a colliery tramway over the Causey Burn. 1727. By Ralph Wood. See p. 120.

The King Edward VII Bridge, Newcastle-upon-Tyne, Tyne and Wear. 1905. By C. A. Harrison. See p. 121.

The Forth Bridge, Lothian. 1883. By Sir John Fowler and Sir Benjamin Baker. See p. 123.

Ribblehead Viaduct, North Yorks. 1869. By John Crossley. See p. 131.

West Finchley, London. Station footbridge.

Hereford and Worcester

Malvern Link Early-twentieth-century example of a station footbridge of bolted steel plates with lattice steel stairs. Corrugated iron roof with decoratively pierced wooden valance.

London

West Finchley An oddity, because when this station was opened by the London and North Eastern Railway in 1933 it was largely made up of parts taken from earlier stations. This open iron lattice footbridge with gracefully arched ends and cast-iron supporting columns was brought from Ryhill station, West Yorkshire, which had been built in 1882 for the Manchester, Sheffield and Lincolnshire Railway (later part of the Great Central) but was closed for passenger traffic (after being renamed Wintersett and Ryhill) in 1930 – see J.N. Young's *Great Northern Suburban*, 1977. West Finchley Station was transferred from the L.N.E.R. to London Transport in 1940.

135

Coulsdon South, Surrey. Station footbridge.

Surrey

Coulsdon South   Iron lattice unroofed footbridge of a type much used around 1880 for stations on the London–Brighton and other Southern lines. Wooden flooring and stairs. Many of this type were afterwards rebuilt in concrete.

Sussex, West

Fishersgate   Similar to the above but extended at either end to give access to the station.

Warwickshire

Nuneaton   Enclosed footbridge incorporated in the architecture of the station, terminating in a brick clock-tower with stone ornaments and a pyramidal roof. Wooden floors and iron stair-rails.

Stratford-upon-Avon Around 1880. Similar to the station footbridge at Taplow (see p. 134) but with the bridge structure of bolted steel plates instead of iron lattice. Enclosed wooden stairs. The next station down the line, Wilmcote, has an equally elegant bridge of the same type but with an unroofed lattice structure.

Wiltshire

Wootton Bassett 1880. Steel plate station footbridge with corrugated iron roof. The stairs, on steel stringers, have half-landings supported on cast-iron columns and ornate cast-iron balusters.

Stratford-upon-Avon, Warwicks. Station footbridge.

7

Suspension Bridges

The principle of the suspension bridge goes back to the most primitive times; to the practice of throwing ropes, initially of plaited creepers and later woven from vegetable fibres, over rivers as a means of crossing them, a practice elaborated in due course to include planks of wood placed crosswise to walk on and additional ropes to hold on to. Such rope bridges are still to be found in mountainous regions in Asia, South America and elsewhere, but suspension bridges did not become part of the constructional repertoire of more advanced bridge builders until the introduction first of iron chains (which were in fact used for this purpose in ancient times in China) and then of woven wire cables. Then, it was found, they could be used to span considerable distances and to provide a level roadway suspended from the chains or cables.

The suspension bridge which set the precedent in relatively modern times for really long spans was the Menai Bridge, thrown over the Menai Strait between North Wales and Anglesey in 1826 as part of an improved London to Holyhead road by Thomas Telford, whose bold inventiveness and versatility as an engineer made, as preceding chapters have shown, so great a contribution to advances in bridge technology. The possibility of bridging the Menai Strait had been discussed for some years previously and John Rennie had designed a three-arch iron bridge for this purpose. Telford followed in 1813 with an iron bridge composed of a single arch of 500-foot span, to be constructed with the help of an ingenious system of suspended centering. This had no backing, but Telford, continuing his own experiments in the use of iron and influenced by Captain Brown's experiments with iron chains (see next page), decided that a suspension bridge was the answer and convinced an interested group of North of England business men that he was right. He was appointed the engineer and work on the Menai Suspension Bridge began in 1819. It spanned the great distance of 580 feet without the need for the intermediate supports of the many-arched types of bridge previously built to span such distances, which inevitably impeded shipping. Its height of over sixty feet above the water allowed quite tall ships to pass beneath it.

Although the Menai Bridge demonstrated to the world both the practical and the dramatic potential of this form of construction, it was not by any means the first of its kind in Britain. Hutchinson's *Antiquities of Durham*, published at Carlisle in 1794, gives an account of a narrow bridge 'for the passage of travellers, but particularly of miners' (they would have been lead-miners) across the Tees, known as the Winch Bridge and linking County Durham with Yorkshire. This bridge was, it appears, built around 1741 and Hutchinson's description of it reads in part:

> About two miles above Middleton, where the river falls in repeated cascades, a bridge suspended on iron chains is stretched from rock to rock over a chasm nearly sixty feet deep ... the bridge is seventy feet in length, and a little more than two feet broad, with a handrail on one side, and planked in such a manner that the traveller experiences all the tremulous motion of the chain, and sees himself suspended over a roaring gulf, on an agitated gang-way, to which few strangers dare trust themselves.

This suspended footbridge, which had wooden flooring laid directly on the cables stretching from bank to bank of the river and diagonal chains underneath as wind-bracing, was taken down in 1802 but its chains are preserved in the Bowes Museum at Barnard Castle. In 1817 two Smith brothers, John (1782–1864) and Thomas (1785–1857), built a small bridge on four suspending chains over the Tweed at Dryburgh, Borders. It has since been demolished. A far more ambitious suspension bridge over the Mersey at Runcorn was designed by Telford in 1813, in conjunction with Captain Brown (1776–1852) of the Royal Navy at the request of a group of Liverpool business men. It was to have had a span as great as 1,000 feet but it was never built; nor was a bridge, also suspended on chains, proposed by the Scottish engineer Robert Stevenson at Cramond near Edinburgh in 1820. In the latter bridge the roadway was to have passed above the chains.

The first large suspension bridge – that is, one carrying a roadway for carriages and wagons – actually to be built was the Union Bridge over the Tweed at Horncliffe, Northumberland, which is still in use. It was completed in 1820 and therefore before Telford's Menai Bridge. The Union Bridge spans 430 feet. Its designer was the same Captain Brown (who had by then retired from the Navy and soon became Sir Samuel Brown) who had been involved at Runcorn. He also designed Brighton Chain Pier which employed a similar chain suspension principle, was completed in 1823 and swept away in a great storm in 1896.

Telford's Menai Bridge was based on the research he and Brown had done

139

for the Runcorn project. After its successful completion in 1826, and the public acclaim it received, suspension bridges were built in some numbers. They included another by Telford at Conway, with its pylons medievalized to accord with the castle close by, the famous Clifton Gorge bridge by Brunel and, at different times during the ensuing hundred or so years, no less than five suspension bridges over the Thames in London: Hammersmith Bridge (1827) by William Tierney Clarke (1783–1852), Hungerford Bridge (1841) by Brunel, Albert Bridge (1873) by R.M. Ordish (1824–86), Lambeth Bridge (1862) by Peter Barlow (1809–85) – replacing a horse ferry (hence the name of the road leading to it) and much criticized at the time for its ugliness – and Chelsea Bridge (1937), replacing one of 1858 by Thomas Page (1803–77) which was not a suspension bridge.

Hungerford Bridge was removed in 1861 to make way for the present rail and footbridge and Hammersmith Bridge was replaced by another suspension bridge (see list at the end of this chapter) in 1887. Lambeth Bridge was rebuilt in 1932. Albert Bridge and Chelsea Bridge still stand as originally built – though in the former case subsequently strengthened.

There were other quite substantial suspension bridges built around this time (see again the list at the end of this chapter) and a good many small private bridges (some of these have already been described in Chapter 3). These were for the most part only for pedestrians, the suspension principle being much favoured in such places because of its lightness and the elegance given it by the catenary form of its cables. Suspension bridges are suitable for road and footbridges only, not for railway bridges on account of the weight and vibration of rail traffic and the fact that the road-deck of a suspension bridge moves to a slight degree. Nevertheless suspended structures must have offered a temptation to the early railway engineers since in their time the capability of suspension bridges to span really long distances had just been established. In fact one railway suspension bridge was constructed by Sir Samuel Brown in 1830. It carried the Stockton–Darlington line over the Tees at Stockton and had a span of 281 feet, but when trains went over it the bridge oscillated dangerously and had to be shored up with timber. It was replaced by an iron bridge by Robert Stephenson in 1842. In America, however, some very long railway suspension bridges have been built and have proved satisfactory because the very great weight of the deck has ensured that no deformation takes place.

The main components of a suspension bridge are the pylons (or towers) to the tops of which the chains or cables are attached, the chains or cables, the hangers (metal rods or cables on which the road-deck is hung) and the road-deck itself. In addition there are usually land-arches carrying the roadway as it approaches the bridge, their extent naturally depending on the nature and steepness of the river banks. In the case of Telford's Menai Bridge the road is carried on a handsome row of 65-foot-high stone arches, like a short viaduct, standing partly on land and partly in the water. Purists have, however, criticized the redundancy of supporting the roadway on these as well as on hangers from the chains above them.

The secure attachment of the landward ends of the chains is of course of the utmost importance. At the Menai Bridge Telford blasted three sloping tunnels 60 feet deep into the rock forming the shore on the Anglesey side of the strait; into these the chains are led and joined together inside a horizontal channel. On the Gwynedd side, where there was no natural rock, he built large masonry blocks in which the ends of the chains are embedded. The pylons here are of relatively simple design, being of stone, made hollow in the upper part for lightness and being pierced by two tiers of twin arches with a small cornice over them.

Other suspension bridges have their pylons treated more elaborately, in a manner derived from some past architectural style. Of such styles the Egyptian was the favourite, and a simplified Egyptian style was employed for the pylons of the most spectacular of all the early suspension bridges, rivalling even the Menai Bridge – spectacular because of its great height (245 feet) above the water and its slender road-deck: the bridge over the Avon Gorge at Clifton near Bristol. This was the subject of a competition held in 1830. Several of the leading engineers of the time entered, including Telford who, moved by one of his periodic romantic impulses, submitted a Gothic design with turreted pylons and with even the chains enriched with fretwork. An engineer of whom little is known, C.H. Capper, submitted a still more romantic design incorporating an artificial medieval ruin. The competition was won by Brunel, then only twenty-four, but owing to lack of funds the bridge was not completed until 1864, just after Brunel's death. In the meantime – from 1843 onwards – an iron bar $1\frac{1}{2}$ ins in diameter was fixed over the gorge between the already completed pylons and passengers were hauled along it in a basket.

The list at the end of this chapter shows that suspension bridges were built intermittently throughout the rest of the nineteenth century. Rather fewer were built in the twentieth century until, with the need to construct improved systems of motor-roads from the 1920s onwards, there was a new interest in this type of structure for crossing wide waterways economically and gracefully. Several suspension bridges of very long span were built in North America at this time although confidence in them was temporarily withheld after the Tacoma Narrows Bridge disaster in 1940. Four months after this 2,800-foot-span bridge in Washington State was completed it started oscillating in a high wind and tore itself to pieces. Too large a degree of flexibility was diagnosed and in later bridges, in Britain as well as in America, the hangers have been made more rigid so as to stiffen the whole structure.

The principal technical development that made the modern generation of suspension bridges – including those in Britain – a practical, economic and aesthetic success was the spinning of cables from steel wire, which had been introduced as an alternative to both chains and bar-cables in France early in the nineteenth century and had been used in most of the great American suspension bridges, notably by John A. Roebling, designer of Brooklyn Bridge, New York (1883). There were also improvements in methods of stiffening the deck to avoid torsion and of preventing undue vibration by inclining the suspender cables. The latter were introduced in the construction of the Severn Bridge (1950–63). They also in this case did away with the need for a stiffening girder.

The new British interest in suspension bridges was thus the beneficiary of American experience, and as a result bridges of the suspension type replaced cantilever bridges for very long spans. After the Second World War several long and impressively light and graceful suspension bridges, incorporating all these structural refinements, were built over major British waterways, notably the Severn Bridge taking the M4 motorway from the West of England into South Wales (completed 1963), the road bridge over the Firth of Forth into Fife at Queensferry (1964), and the Humber Bridge across the estuary of that name connecting Lincolnshire with Humberside (1980). The last, with a span of 4,625 feet, is still, at the time of writing, the longest single-span bridge in the world.

A Selection of Suspension Bridges, listed by Counties (by Regions in Scotland)

ENGLAND

Avon

Aust Severn Bridge, linking the West of England with South Wales. Opened 1963 as a toll-bridge. By Sir Gilbert Roberts (1899–1978) of Freeman, Fox and Partners. Rectangular steel-frame pylons 400 feet high. Main span of 3,240 feet (total length including side spans 5,240 feet). Road-deck in the form of a hollow steel box 75 feet wide and 10 feet deep from which cycle-tracks and footways are cantilevered a further 30 feet. Roadway 120 feet above the water. Its stability in high winds called in question since the introduction of heavier goods vehicles. The M4 motorway continues on the Welsh side over a second bridge across the Wye which joins the Severn at this point. Designed by the same engineers, it is a cable-stayed steel bridge with a single cable over central pylons and box-girder steel deck.

Clifton Bridge, Avon. Over the Avon gorge. 1836–64. By I. K. Brunel.

Clifton over the Avon   1836–64. By Brunel. 702-foot span between the pylons which are of stone, each 86 feet high and pierced by one segmental and one rounded arch. Roadway 245 feet above water level. The wrought-iron chains, composed of links 25 feet long bolted together, were taken from the old Hungerford suspension bridge over the Thames in London, designed by Brunel in 1845 and demolished in 1861. The completion of the bridge, five years after Brunel's death, was supervised by W.H. Barlow and Sir John Hawkshaw (1811–91). On the inner face of the pylon on the Clifton side is an inscription which reads *Suspensa Vix Via Fit*, presumably an allusion to the long time that elapsed between design and completion.

Buckinghamshire

Marlow   1829. By William Tierney Clarke who also designed the famous suspension bridge at Budapest, Hungary. Replaced a medieval bridge destroyed in the Civil War, rebuilt in 1642 and destroyed again in 1789. Strengthened 1862. Marlow Bridge is the only vehicular suspension bridge over the

Marlow Bridge, Bucks. Over the Thames. 1829. By William Tierney Clarke.

Thames except those in London. 217 feet between pylons, which are of stone with semi-circular arches and Classical details. Wrought-iron suspension chains painted white and cross-girders carrying timber decking.

Cheshire

Chester   Footbridge over the Dee leading to Queen's Park. 1923, replacing a similar bridge of 1852. By Charles Greenwood, City Engineer. 275-foot span. Steel framed pylons; wire cables; deck of timber on steel girders with lattice-girder parapets.

Cornwall

Tamar Road Bridge over the river of that name, close to Brunel's Royal Albert railway bridge (see page 119)   A toll-bridge replacing a ferry and the first road bridge to link Plymouth with Cornwall. 1959. By Mott, Hay and Anderson. Reinforced concrete, with rectangular framed piers on either bank of the river continued upwards to form plain rectangular pylons. Concrete deck supported on welded steel stiffening trusses 16 feet deep. Galvanized wire cables anchored into the natural rock. Central span 1,100 feet.

Derbyshire

Buxton over the Goyt west of the town   Late nineteenth century. Twin trellised iron pylons, arched between. Trellised railings. Painted white.

Hereford and Worcester

Hereford   Victoria Footbridge over the Wye south of Castle Green. 1898. Deck of iron beams. Arched iron lattice pylons with pinnacles and a coat of arms. Lattice handrails. Stone piers. Main span 80 feet; narrow side spans. Lamps at either end on ornamental stone pedestals.

Victoria Footbridge, Hereford. Over the Wye. 1898.

145

Albert Bridge, Chelsea, London. Over the Thames. 1873. By R. M. Ordish.

Humberside

Kingston-upon-Hull   Humber Bridge over the estuary of that name, four miles west of Hull. 1972. By Freeman, Fox and Partners. Concrete pylons consisting of twin vertical members with horizontal bracing between. Steel woven wire cables. Total length 7,280 feet. Clearance above high water 98 feet. Span between pylons 4,625 feet, making this the longest suspension bridge in the world. The next longest in Europe is the Tagus Bridge at Lisbon (3,320 feet) and in America the longest is the Verrezano Heights Bridge, New York (4,260 feet).

146

London

Albert Bridge, Chelsea, over the Thames 1873 (a toll-bridge until 1879; strengthened 1884). By R.M. Ordish, who patented a 'straight chain suspension' system for bridge construction in 1858 and who also designed the roof of the Albert Hall. 711 feet long in three spans; 450 feet between the iron pylons which are 101 feet above high water and embellished with tiers of iron columns. A complicated spider's-web-like network of chains and hangers but not a true suspension bridge since the road-deck is partly supported on cantilevers. The chain anchorages are housed in small octagonal pavilions with pointed roofs. The bridge is beautifully illuminated after dark.

Hammersmith Bridge over the Thames 1887. By Sir Joseph Bazalgette (1819–91), engineer to the Metropolitan Board of Works and designer also of Battersea and Putney Bridges. Replaced the suspension bridge of 1827 by W.T. Clarke. Highly ornamented; arched pylons with spindly turrets on top and giant volutes at the foot of the secondary pylons to which the suspension chains are anchored. At present all painted yellow.

Northumberland

Horncliffe Union Bridge over the Tweed. 1820 (the first large suspension bridge). By Sir Samuel Brown. 360-foot span. Twelve wrought-iron chains. Only one stone pylon 60 feet high, the chains at the other end being attached to the rock face of the river bank. The bridge was strengthened in 1903 when steel cables were added.

Shropshire

Shrewsbury Porthill Bridge over the Rea Brook. 1922. A steel footbridge nicely sited but of rather primitive construction for so recent a date.

Tyne and Wear

Newcastle-upon-Tyne Scotswood suspension bridge over the Tyne. 1829 (widened 1931). By John Green (1787–1852). Stone pylons with projecting upper storeys supported on brackets. 353-foot span between pylons. Wrought-iron suspension chains (replaced in 1931 by steel-wire cables) supporting steel girders and timber decking.

Yorkshire, North

Huttons Ambo south-west of Malton   Footbridge over the Derwent leading to the now-closed railway station. 1886. 95-foot span. Triangular pylons made from old railway lines.

Middleham over the Ure   1829. By Edward Welch (1806–68) and Joseph Aloysius Hansom (1803–82) who were partners until 1849, after which Hansom founded the *Builder* magazine and invented the cab called by his name.

WALES

Gwent

Newport   Transporter bridge over the Usk. 1906. By F. Arnodin, the French engineer who, the year before, had built the more famous transporter bridge at Marseille which was destroyed in the Second World War. A steel girder 177 feet above the water spans 645 feet and is supported on cables suspended from steel towers 241 feet high. Passengers and vehicles cross the river on a flat carriage hung from the girder. It is one of two surviving transporter bridges in Britain, the other, at Middlesbrough (see page 176), not being of suspension construction.

Newport, Gwent. Transporter bridge over the Usk. 1906. By F. Arnodin.

Conway Bridge, Gwynedd. 1826. By Thomas Telford.

Gwynedd

Conway over the river of the same name   1826 (replacing a ferry). By Telford. Now the property of the National Trust. 327-foot span between stone pylons, which have battlemented turrets and machicolations over a segmental arch to harmonize with the medieval castle close by. In Telford's own words: 'the bridge, which is right opposite the water-entrance of the castle, has the appearance of a huge drawbridge with an embanked approach or causeway.' Eight chains. Strengthened in 1912 by the addition of extra cables and cross girders and supplemented in 1958 by a new road-bridge alongside because the arches of Telford's pylons are so narrow that they could take only one-way traffic.

Menai Suspension Bridge over the Menai Strait to Anglesey, a toll-bridge until 1945   1818–26. By Telford. 580 feet between pylons, which are of stone, tapered, and are approached by arched stone viaducts – three arches of

149

Cambus O'May footbridge, Ballater, Grampian. Over the Dee. 1905.

52-foot span on the south side and four on the north. Double roadway 100 feet above high-water level supported on sixteen chains each composed of thirty-six half-inch square wrought-iron links alternately long and short. Parapets renewed with a steel lattice railing in 1906. The bridge was strengthened in 1906 and has undergone several subsequent restorations involving replacement of the chains and the provision of a new deck. These have necessarily somewhat coarsened the lines of Telford's original structure. Traffic on the A5 to Holyhead now uses the new roadway incorporated in the Britannia railway bridge (see page 122) when it was reconstructed in 1970.

SCOTLAND

Borders

Melrose Gattonside footbridge over the Tweed north-west of the town. 1826 (restored 1928). By the Redpath Brown engineering company. 300-foot span. 4 ft 6 ins wide. Two pairs of chains composed of 10-foot-long iron rods. Wooden deck. Imposing Gothic-style pylons 24 feet high.

The Severn Bridge, Avon and Gwent. 1963. By Sir Gilbert Roberts. See p. 142.

Hammersmith Bridge, London. Over the Thames. 1887. By Sir Joseph Bazalgette. See p. 147.

Union Bridge, Horncliffe, Northumberland. Over the Tweed. 1820. By Sir Samuel Brown. See p. 147.

Menai Bridge, Gwynedd. 1818. By Thomas Telford. See p. 149.

Grampian

Ballater Cambus O'May Bridge. Narrow footbridge over the Dee. 1905. Lattice steel pylons. Trellised iron railing. Painted white.

Highland

Inverness over the Ness 1852. Replaced a stone bridge swept away in a flood in 1849. By J.M. Rendel (1799–1856), a pupil of Telford but chiefly known for his docks and harbours. 225 feet between the stone pylons, which are battlemented and pierced by segmental arches. Wrought-iron chains and girder supporting the deck.

Lothian

East Calder in Almondell Country Park 1966. By James Morris (born 1931) and R. Steedman (born 1929). Footway suspended from cables attached to a single pylon.

Forth Road Bridge, South Queensferry, Lothian. 1959. By Mott, Hay and Anderson.

Forth Road Bridge over the Firth of Forth at South Queensferry 1959. By Mott, Hay and Anderson; consulting architects, Giles Gilbert Scott and Partners. 512-foot-high pylons of welded steel plate with diagonal bracing between the vertical members. Open lattice-steel deck. Main span of 3,300 feet. Total length including side spans 5,980 feet.

Strathclyde

Glasgow Portland Street footbridge over the Clyde. 1851. By Alexander Kirkland, architect, and George Martin, engineer. Replaced a bridge (not a suspension bridge) of 1836 by Robert Stevenson which became unsafe after the removal of a nearby weir in 1842. Reconstructed 1871. Grecian-style arched pylons in stone. Double suspension chains of flat links support a light lattice-girder deck spanning 414 feet.

St Andrew's Bridge, Glasgow. Over the Clyde. 1854. By Neil Robson.

Glasgow St Andrew's Bridge over the Clyde to Glasgow Green. 1854 (restored 1905). By Neil Robson (1807–69). Replaced a ferry. Cast iron with double chains; stiffened by a lattice-girder. Pylons designed by Charles O'Neill, in the form of Corinthian gateways with paired columns also in cast iron, full entablatures and low-pitched roofs. Span 220 feet. Width 13 feet. For pedestrians only, who were charged a toll during the bridge's first years.

8

Footbridges

There are plenty of interesting footbridges in England, Wales and Scotland, some of which have already been described in the preceding chapters: elegant light suspension bridges over streams and rivers (Chapter 7); bridges by which one may cross the line at railway stations (Chapter 6); small bridges – plain or fanciful – in the parks of country houses (Chapter 3). Moreover some of the earliest of the medieval bridges described in Chapter 1 – clapper bridges – could also be described as footbridges since they were built for men or animals to cross on foot. The same applies to packhorse bridges, but these are often quite substantial. In the ordinary sense of the word a footbridge is light and narrow.

Many are anonymous and of much the same pattern, especially footbridges over streams in the countryside; so only a few examples are given in the list at the end of this chapter to represent the various types commonly to be found. The simplest, such as those over millstreams and mill-races, are generally of wood since they do not have to bear heavy loads, and some consist of no more than a narrow wooden deck and a plain handrail. In contrast to these, the limited role of a footbridge does not prevent it from sometimes being the occasion for architectural display as many of the bridges in private parks, designed as eye-catching incidents in the landscape, have already shown.

Perhaps the most varied array of footbridges having some architectural pretensions is to be seen at Cambridge. Here a line of colleges backs on to the Cam, and from their rear entrances footbridges – no doubt used at one time by horse-riders also – cross that river and lead to paths across the water-meadows beyond – known as the Backs – and eventually to a motor-road. They range in style from the eccentric 'mathematical' timber bridge at Queens' College to the Classical three-arched stone bridge, a monument in miniature, at Clare; from the covered neo-Gothic bridge at St John's to the modern Garret Hostel bridge. Most are eighteenth- or early-nineteenth-century, but the one at Clare College (1629) is the oldest bridge in Cambridge, though only because all the river

Clare College, Cambridge. Over the Cam. 1639. By Thomas Grumbold.

bridges in the city were demolished during the Civil War except one – the Great Bridge, as it was then called (now better known as Magdalene Bridge) – and this was replaced by an iron bridge in 1813. Only one of the fascinating line of bridges along the Backs was originally of iron: the Garret Hostel Bridge between Clare and Trinity Colleges, designed in 1835 by William Mylne (1781–1863) the son of the noted bridge architect Robert Mylne – see page 33. It was single-arched with railings ornamented with Gothic tracery in cast iron. It was demolished in 1959 and replaced by the concrete bridge described on page 160.

To the structural materials referred to in the preceding pages – brick, stone, iron and timber – a new addition has been made in recent years: reinforced concrete, the early development of which is recounted in the next chapter.

Concrete, and especially prestressed concrete, has been used to create footbridges as satisfactory as any. Among these are pedestrian crossings over motorways where, as in the case of many of the road bridges over motorways and the flyovers that form part of them – again see the next chapter – the capacity of reinforced concrete to achieve muscularity combined with elegance, a sense of fulfilling the functions of a bridge with no unnecessary fuss, has been fully exploited.

Besides the motorway footbridges there are two others in reinforced concrete that deserve special attention. One is the footbridge that leaps over the Wear at Durham in a single graceful span to link the rock on which the cathedral and the central buildings of the university stand with Dunelm House, the university students' community building, on the opposite river bank. It was designed in 1963 by one of the most eminent contemporary engineers, Sir Ove Arup (born 1895), who throughout his career has specialized in concrete. The

Kingsgate footbridge, Durham, linking Dunelm House to the cathedral rock. 1963. By Sir Ove Arup.

other, unusually, is neither by an engineer nor an architect but by a painter, Victor Pasmore (born 1908). In 1954 Pasmore was called in by the general manager of one of the post-war new towns, Peterlee, also in County Durham, as a consultant on the design of one of the town's housing neighbourhoods. Within this neighbourhood is a small park containing a lake. Pasmore designed a footbridge over it, conceived as an abstract work of sculpture that would provide a focal point in what might have appeared otherwise as no more than a featureless expanse of grass; also as a shelter and play area for children. The Peterlee bridge is in many ways a modern equivalent of the bridges that embellish the parks of eighteenth-century country houses.

These two, and the bridges along the Backs at Cambridge, are however exceptional. The normal role of a footbridge is to cross a river, stream or highway as simply and economically as possible. This still allows it to fill the role of an agreeable object in the landscape, as the best of the recent motorway footbridges amply demonstrate.

A Selection of Footbridges, listed by Counties (by Regions in Scotland)

(*others listed under Private and Ornamental Bridges, Railway Bridges and Suspension Bridges*)

ENGLAND

Berkshire

Maidenhead over a stream of the Thames connecting a small public park (once the grounds of the Guards Boat Club) on the west bank to an island Nineteenth century (precise date and designer unknown). Iron supported on wood piers. Four elliptical arches with decoratively pierced spandrels. Wooden deck and steps at either end. Iron handrail.

Buckinghamshire

Boveney over a channel of a Thames lock, upstream from Windsor   Date and designer unknown. Wood, with a slightly bowed deck supported on pairs of raking struts. Painted white.

Cambridgeshire

Cambridge over the Cam: bridges along the Backs.

QUEENS' COLLEGE   1749. By William Etheridge (died 1776), but erected by James Essex (1722–84), who began as a carpenter but did much architectural work for Cambridge colleges. A wooden bridge, pegged together without the use of nails and called the 'mathematical' bridge because it was claimed that its design would permit any of its timbers to be removed without disturbing the whole. Said to be modelled on a design by Palladio. It was rebuilt in teak in 1902 but to the original design.

KING'S COLLEGE   1818. By William Wilkins (1778–1839). Stone. One segmental arch. Solid parapet. Restrained Classical detail.

CLARE COLLEGE   1639. Said to have been designed by Thomas Grumbold (died 1657), one of a family of masons – see below – who worked much at Cambridge, but its ambitious style – it was the city's first Classical bridge – suggests that if he constructed it he had some professional architectural guidance. Stone. Three segmental arches with cutwaters between. Balustraded parapet with pedestals at intervals decorated with carved panels. Stone spheres on top of each. Total span 80 feet.

TRINITY COLLEGE   1763 (replaced a seventeenth-century bridge). By James Essex. Stone. Three segmental arches with prominent moulded rings. Solid parapet elegantly curled at the ends.

ST JOHN'S COLLEGE   Old Bridge. 1696–1712. By Robert Grumbold (1639–1720) but based on suggestions put forward by Sir Christopher Wren. Stone. Three segmental arches. Parapet with square balusters. At the college end a stone-pillared gateway also by Grumbold.

ST JOHN'S COLLEGE   New Bridge. 1827. Covered bridge in Perpendicular Gothic by William Hutchinson (1779–1869). Sometimes called the Bridge of Sighs after the footbridge called so at the Doge's Palace in Venice. Stone. One

'Mathematical' wooden bridge at Queens' College, Cambridge. 1749. By William Etheridge.

Garret Hostel Bridge, Cambridge. Over the Cam. 1959. By Guy Morgan.

low segmental arch. Lit by four traceried windows separated by buttresses ending in pinnacles. Battlemented parapets between the latter.

GARRET HOSTEL BRIDGE across the Cam at the end of Garret Hostel Lane between Trinity College and Trinity Hall   1959. By Guy Morgan (born 1902) and T.V. Burrows, Cambridge City Engineer. Prestressed concrete with a bush-hammered finish. One flat segmental arch of 85 foot span. York stone abutments. Iron railings.

Godmanchester   'Chinese' bridge between the town hall and the grammar school, leading to an island in the Ouse. 1827 (rebuilt to same design in 1869 and 1960). By James Gallier (1798–1866). Timber. One segmental arch with diagonal cross-bracing in the spandrels. Handrail of vertical posts, the panels between filled with a pattern in the 'Chinese taste' made fashionable by the eighteenth-century furniture maker Thomas Chippendale, but an unexpectedly late use of this style.

Cheshire

Beeston giving access over the moat to the inner ward of the thirteenth-century castle ruins, previously inaccessible since the demolition of the medieval draw-bridge 1975. By A.B.E. Clark of the Department of the Environment. The reinforced concrete footbridge springs in one upward-sloping arc of 66 feet from the rocky edge of the outer ward into the castle gateway. The concrete was delivered to this difficult site ready mixed and pumped into place. Iron railings.

Derbyshire

Matlock Bath 1887 (built to commemorate Queen Victoria's Jubilee). Iron. Single bow arch.

Durham

Durham Kingsgate Footbridge over the Wear, linking the university buildings surrounding Palace Green on the cathedral rock with the students'

Beeston, Cheshire. Footbridge over the moat into the gateway of the thirteenth-century castle. 1975. By A.B.E. Clark.

Bourton-on-the-Water, Glos. 1756.

community building, Dunelm House. 1963. By Sir Ove Arup. Reinforced concrete. 337 feet long, 11 feet wide and 47 feet above water level. The trough-like deck, forming a box-beam, is supported by pairs of V-shaped concrete struts springing from the banks of the river. So as not to obstruct river traffic during construction the bridge was built in two halves parallel to each bank and, when completed, swung into position and the halves locked together by bronze expansion joints.

Hamsterley (west of Bishop Auckland) Sills Bridge over Bedburn Beck. 1956. By W.H.B. Cotton, County Bridge Engineer. Concrete, of precast units prestressed together on erection. 54-foot span with a slight upward curve between stone abutments. The bridge was prefabricated on the river bank and launched across it on temporary scaffolding. Iron railings.

Peterlee over a lake at Sunny Blunts, a housing estate in the south-west area of the new town   1970. By the painter Victor Pasmore. Reinforced concrete. Two-level covered area in centre. Iron railings.

Gloucestershire

Bibury over the Coln   Eighteenth century. Three stone arches.

Bourton-on-the-Water   Narrow Bridge. 1756. Hump-backed with minimal parapets. Three low arches of heavily rusticated stone.

Hampshire

Basingstoke over the M3 motorway at Hatch, just east of the town   1970. By H.N. Jenner, Hampshire County Surveryor. Reinforced concrete. The main 120-foot span over the roadway has a suspended central section between side sections cantilevered from concrete columns on the sloping verges. Spiral approach ramps. Aluminium railings.

Whitchurch over a stream of the Test   Date and designer unknown. Wood. Narrow with wooden handrail. Unpainted. A typically plain but picturesque rural footbridge.

Kent

Swanscombe over the A2   1964. By J.A. Bergg and H. Bowdler, Kent County Surveyor. An exceptionally elegant example of the reinforced concrete high-

Swanscombe, Kent. Concrete footbridge over the A2. 1964. By J.A. Bergg and H. Bowdler.

way footbridge. One three-hinged arch spanning 160 feet with a prestressing tendon passing through it. Cantilevered side spans. Iron railings.

Lancashire

Hindley House over the Preston Bypass on the M6 motorway 1957. By Sir James Drake, Lancashire County Surveyor. Two precast reinforced concrete arch members meeting in the centre of the single 165-foot span. Precast concrete planks form the footway. The sloping ends have concrete steps cast *in situ*. Iron railings.

Wycoller (a hamlet east of Colne, near the Yorkshire border) Date unknown. The most primitive possible stone bridge: a single slab spanning outcrops of rock on either bank of a small stream. Nearby over the same stream are a two-span clapper bridge and a two-arch packhorse bridge as well as a ford crossed by stepping-stones.

Wycoller, Lancs. Two primitive types of bridge over a stream.

Lincolnshire

Boston (near) over the West Fen Drain   1811 (marked with date and 'cast at Butterley'). One segmental cast-iron arch between stone abutments. Iron railings.

London

St James's Park over the lake   1956. By the architect's department, Ministry of Works. Replaced an iron suspension bridge of 1857 designed by Sir Matthew Digby Wyatt (1805–86) which, it was claimed, had become unsafe. Reinforced concrete. Three flat segmental arches, the centre one wider. Haunches inscribed with outline figures of fish by the sculptor John Skeaping. Iron railings. The park, which was first enclosed by Henry VIII and replanted, improved and eventually opened to the public by Charles II, was laid out in its present form by John Nash in 1825. Famous view eastwards to the Whitehall skyline.

Northumberland

Ovingham over the Tyne ten miles west of Newcastle, leading to Prudhoe   Nineteenth century (precise date and designer unknown). Iron. Very narrow, on a row of circular cast-iron columns arranged in pairs, each sloping to meet at deck level, with thin cross-bracing between. Iron railings. There are several footbridges of similar construction elsewhere in the county.

Nottinghamshire

Newark over the Trent   1915. An early use of reinforced concrete. Single arch with a span of 90 feet and less than 6 ins thick at the crown.

Oxfordshire

Fiddler's Island over a stream of the Thames just above Oxford   1865. Iron. One pair of lattice arches supporting a wooden deck and serving also as a handrail.

Oxford over the Isis, carrying the tow-path across the river near Salter's boat-yard alongside Folly Bridge   1952. By Donovan H. Lee for the Thames Conservancy. Replaced a three-span wooden bridge of 1884. Prestressed concrete. The main span of 33 feet between twin-pillared concrete piers consists of two balanced cantilevers meeting at the centre. Width 6 ft 6 ins. Iron railings.

Yorkshire, West

Silsden, on the edge of Rombalds Moor, over a small water-course often dry   Date unknown. Stone. One elliptical arch. Exceptionally narrow for an arched bridge; width between parapets only 18 ins.

WALES

Gwent

St Mellons over the A48 between Cardiff and Newport   1964. A standard pattern of pedestrian overpass for busy motor-roads furnished by the Ministry of Transport. Related in style (somewhat clumsily) to some of the passenger footbridges at railway stations – see Chapter 6. Precast reinforced concrete. Stairs at either end of concrete cast *in situ*. Iron railings. There is a similar standard pattern in steel.

SCOTLAND

Borders

Galashiels over the Gala Water   1954. By Blyth and Blyth. Reinforced concrete. Because one side of the river is much higher than the other, and because there is also a railway line to be crossed on the higher bank, the bridge is on two levels, connected by a double spiral staircase within a hollow 10-foot-diameter reinforced concrete tower at the river's edge. Each span is 58 feet but that over the railway line has twin central supports. The decks of prestressed concrete also carry sewage pipes from a nearby housing estate. Iron railings with wire-mesh panels.

Maidenhead, Berks. Iron and wood footbridge from a public park to an island in the Thames. Nineteenth century. *See p. 157.*

New Bridge at St John's College, Cambridge. Over the Cam. 1827. By William Hutchinson. *See p. 159.*

Godmanchester, Cambs. 'Chinese' bridge leading to an island in the Ouse. 1827. By James Gallier. See p. 160.

Peterlee New Town, Co. Durham. Concrete footbridge, partly covered, in a park in the Sunny Blunts housing estate. 1970. By Victor Pasmore. See p. 162.

Galashiels, Borders. Two-level concrete footbridge over the Gala Water. 1954. By Blyth and Blyth.

Roxburgh over the Tweed just outside the village   1850. Attached to the side of a three-arch stone railway bridge, the piers of which have projections on the downstream side built to carry the footbridge. This is of iron with fish-shaped trusses supporting each 50-foot span, the upper element being a flat strip of cast iron and the lower one a bar of wrought iron. Between them are V-shaped cast-iron struts. Railing of iron rods. Decking wood. This is an unusual form of construction similar to that of the Gaunless Bridge in County Durham – the first iron railway bridge now in the National Railway Museum at York (see page 109) – the main difference being that each span of the Roxburgh bridge is bowed upwards because of the shape of the trusses, with the result that the surface of the deck forms a succession of curves.

9

New Styles, Techniques and Purposes: the Last Hundred Years

Most of the bridges discussed in this chapter are road bridges since the canal- and railway-building eras were over by the 1880s. They embrace the many types of structure, old and new, employed during the last hundred years except suspension bridges and footbridges, both of which the preceding chapters have recorded up to the present day. The new developments here to be discussed are of three main kinds: changes in style due to the evolution of architectural taste, changes in purpose and changes in structural technique, in the case of the last most notably the changes brought about by the introduction of reinforced concrete and, in due course, of prestressed concrete.

To begin, however, with the changes in taste of the last hundred years, it will have been noted that the early-nineteenth-century bridges described in Chapter 2 remained, when they had any monumental pretentions, faithful on the whole to the Classical idiom established by seventeenth- and eighteenth-century architects. There were only occasional hints, as in Telford's castellated bridge at Tongueland, Dumfries and Galloway (see page 57), of more romantic aspirations – which were to be expected seeing that the beginnings of the Industrial Revolution overlapped in time with the Romantic Movement – and of the approach of the Gothic Revival which was to play so dominant a part in nineteenth-century architecture. The Gothic Revival did not in the case of bridges transform the whole architectural vocabulary, as it did in many kinds of building, because structural logic demands that bridges, whatever the vagaries of style they may be subjected to, preserve their basic form. Nothing can deprive a bridge of its unique architectural attribute: that it is the only kind of building not made of glass of which it is possible to perceive the inside and the outside simultaneously.

Yet the more romantic and picturesque styles, and the great variety of periods and countries from which the later nineteenth-century architects drew inspiration, were reflected at least in the embellishment of many bridges and in a few instances determined their whole architectural character. We do not have to go outside London to find examples. Hammersmith Bridge – see Chapter 7 – is a typical instance of a bridge heavily ornamented in the later Victorian taste, but perhaps the most whole-hearted instance of this, and the best known, is Tower Bridge with its battlemented wing-walls and other features conceived by the City Corporation's architect Sir Horace Jones (1819–87) as appropriate neighbours to the adjoining medieval fortress, the Tower of London. In the same way Telford medievalized his Conway suspension bridge to harmonize with the nearby castle, and when Westminster Bridge was rebuilt in 1854 (by Thomas Page under the aesthetic guidance of Sir Charles Barry) it was given trefoil-ornamented spandrels and parapets to harmonize with the Houses of Parliament.

Tower Bridge was, however, more consciously conceived as a public monument, and its medieval style was a requirement of the Government of the day (who also required that the bridge should be armed with cannon, but these were not installed until a generation after it was built and then in very different circumstances from those envisaged – see page 179). No sooner was Tower Bridge completed (in 1894) than it became the picture-postcard symbol of the tourist's London, just as its almost exact contemporary, the Eiffel Tower (1889) became the symbol of Paris, and the Statue of Liberty (1886), another monument of the same epoch, the symbol of New York.

The picturesque architectural costume in which Tower Bridge is apparelled must not be allowed to distract our attention from the highly practical, and – at the time it was built – technically advanced, nature of its design. It was an ambitious example of a bascule bridge; that is, one in which the roadway can be raised and lowered to allow the passage of shipping on the same principle as the drawbridges that allowed or disputed access to the gateways of medieval castles. But instead of hand-operated winches, the bascules of Tower Bridge, of which there are a pair meeting in the centre, can be raised – in one and a half minutes – by hydraulic machinery housed within the two towers. The bascules are now seldom raised (except as a show for tourists at times published in advance) since few large ships go so far up-river, and they have become part of a busy and almost permanently available highway. Yet the passage over the point where the two bascules meet can still be felt as a sudden jolt when a vehicle passes over it.

Tower Bridge is thus at the same time aesthetically an example of Victorian taste and technically an example of a river bridge functioning in a new way typical of this era when engineers had acquired the mechanical as well as the structural expertise that enabled them to put forward a variety of similar contrivances. But before the bascule bridge just described was decided upon in 1885 as the best means of providing a badly-needed river crossing without impeding shipping, a succession of projects with the same purpose and for the same point on the Thames had been devised from 1872 onwards, each to be rejected in its turn. The first was a proposal by R.M. Ordish for a two-span toll-bridge supplemented by four tunnels. This was followed in 1876 by proposals for another similar bridge, for another tunnel, for a platform running on rails laid on the bed of the river, on which vehicles would be carried from one side to the other, for a similar platform rolling between six piers planted at intervals across the width of the river – this idea was put forward by Sir George Bruce (1821-1908), Robert Stephenson's assistant on several of his railway enterprises – for a steam ferry and for a high-level bridge with hydraulic lifts for vehicles at each end.

In 1878 Sir Joseph Bazalgette produced several designs for Tower Bridge, one of which, for a single-span steel bridge, 850 feet long with a clearance of 60 feet above the water, got as far as consideration by Parliament but was rejected because shipping interests thought this amount of clearance insufficient. Later the same year Sir Horace Jones proposed a bascule bridge and this (see page 198) was only rejected because the bascules were not designed to open fully and therefore left too narrow a passage for shipping. After further proposals for a cantilever bridge and for a tunnel had been put forward in 1870 and 1883 the City Corporation decided in 1885 that Sir Horace Jones's notion of a bascule bridge was still the best and appointed Sir John Wolfe Barry as the engineer, to work with Jones as architect. It was Barry who suggested a horizontal footway between the towers high enough to allow the bascules to open fully in place of Jones's arched span. The final scheme was approved by Parliament later in 1885.

This lengthy process of trial and error may have been exceptional, but the Thames was not the only river on which engineers exercised their ingenuity in aid of a similar purpose. Two further instances, in which different means were devised for allowing the passage of ships along an inland waterway while only temporarily interrupting traffic over it (to be compared with the so-called telescope bridge carrying a railway line over the Arun described already in Chapter 6), are the swing bridge and the much more recent lift bridge. A relatively small cast-iron swing bridge with a span of 45 feet was built at St Katharine's Dock, London, as far back as 1818 and there were others in the London Docks and on the Caledonian Canal. The steel swing bridge over the Tyne at Newcastle (page 183), built in 1876, has two openings for shipping, each of 110 feet. A lift bridge is designed to be raised bodily. That at Middlesbrough (page 177), built in 1934, can be lifted 120 feet clear of the water. An even more spectacular invention than these was the transporter bridge, a vast but remarkably light steel framework erected over a waterway from which a platform was slung to carry passengers and vehicles from one side to the other. Three of these have been built in Britain, at Runcorn over the Mersey, at Newport over the Usk and at Middlesbrough over the Tees. Only the first no longer exists; it was replaced by a steel arch bridge (see page 176) in 1956. The second, being constructed on the suspension principle (as was the one at Runcorn), has already been noted in Chapter 7. For the Middlesbrough transporter bridge, also see page 176.

One other, and even more recent, new structural technique employing steel should be mentioned here: that employed in the Bailey Bridge invented during the Second World War by Sir Donald C. Bailey (born 1901), an engineer then working for the British Ministry of Supply, who was knighted for this achievement. Its purpose was temporarily to replace bridges blown up or destroyed by bombing. It was assembled out of prefabricated interchangeable trussed steel panels, each 10 feet long and designed so that it could be handled by six men. A Bailey Bridge could span up to 240 feet.

In spite of being responsible for the several technical innovations just described, neither the end of the nineteenth century nor the beginning of the twentieth were great bridge-building eras. Britain's road system was already well equipped with bridges (a great many of which, however, were widened during this period) and the canal-building and railway-building eras were long past. But in the mid-twentieth-century the increasing use and quantity of motor transport led to a vast programme of building bridges with a new purpose – the second of the changes occurring in modern times referred to at the beginning of this chapter. This new purpose was that of serving the system of motorways which was superimposed on the English, and to a lesser degree on the Welsh and Scottish, road systems from the late 1950s onwards.

One basic principle of the motorway was to provide arterial highways free from the hazards of road intersections. When the new motorways crossed the existing road system the old roads passed over them on bridges, or sometimes under them, the connection being made by means of slip roads. Travelling along a motorway therefore, the eye is met by an unprecedented succession of newly constructed bridges. To take but one example, building the twenty-seven-mile stretch of the M6 motorway between junction 13, south of Stafford, and junction 16, on the Cheshire border east of Crewe, involved the construction of seventy-five new bridges: thirty over or under existing roads, four over railways (including a viaduct across the Sow valley carrying the motorway over the river, the railway and a peat bog), nine others over streams, twenty-one to preserve access between parts of farms severed by the motorway, ten for pedestrians to cross and one at a service area. In many parts of the country, notably at the points where motorways themselves intersect, what may still be categorized as bridges are enlarged to become great elevated structures, vast in their scale and complexity, imposing themselves on several acres of the landscape.

Motorway bridges and overpasses are almost invariably of reinforced concrete, the most important of the new techniques referred to at the beginning of this chapter. By its use the motorways of the 1960s and after have been furnished with some of the handsomest bridges of modern times if we except the two or three recent suspension bridges noted at the end of Chapter 7. Earlier structural techniques of course continued in use, especially steel for many of the railway bridges over motorways, and a number of fine new bridges in other materials than concrete have been built during this century as the list at the end of this chapter demonstrates. But with the exception of those built of concrete they represent no radical departure from the methods employed by nineteenth-century engineers.

Although concrete is by no means a twentieth-, or even a nineteenth-century invention (the Romans not only used mass concrete but used it for arched structures such as the Colosseum and the dome of the Pantheon), its scientific use may be said to date first from the invention of Portland cement by Joseph Aspdin in 1824 and then from a number of experiments by French engineers later in the nineteenth century. It was these that led to the development of reinforced concrete – concrete with steel rods inserted in the places where tensile (as distinct from compressive) strength is required. An English engineer, Sir William Fairbairn (1789–1874), had used a primitive form of reinforced concrete in a refinery at Manchester as early as 1845 and a Newcastle builder, William Wilkinson, took out a patent for a similar type of structure in 1854; but the significant experiments leading to the use of reinforced concrete as we know it were all French. Most notable were those of François Hennebique (1842–1921) who first employed it in 1879. In 1898 he designed the first large-scale reinforced concrete bridge, the Pont de Chatellerault, with a span of 172 feet.

Just before this one of Hennebique's assistants, L. G. Mouchel (1852–1908), moved to Britain and set up an office at Swansea where a reinforced concrete flour-mill was built under his supervision in 1897 (demolished 1983), but no reinforced concrete bridges were built in Britain until several years later, unless one counts Flixton Bridge at Homersfield, Suffolk, a small bridge of concrete with a cast-iron frame embedded in it. This was built in 1870 and demolished exactly a hundred years later. Another structure of some historic interest is the Glenfinnan railway viaduct, Highland, built of mass concrete in 1897 and still standing – see page 131.

The first reinforced concrete bridge in Britain using techniques resembling those of today was built at Chewton Glen in the New Forest in 1901 and a somewhat larger one, with a single span of 44 feet, at Satterthwaite, Cumbria, in 1902. But until concrete came into common use for bridges after about 1920, it was employed for the most part either for strengthening existing stone or brick bridges, for widening them or for building new bridges in a form closely resembling that of the traditional arched bridge. Concrete had not yet evolved a recognizable idiom of its own. Its advantages, however, had become clear. Among them, in addition to the slenderness of outline that emerged when engineers began to appreciate the aesthetic potentialities of the material's innate strength (see for example the 1915 footbridge at Nottingham – page 165), were economy in the use of skilled labour and in the transport of heavy ingredients like steel, which was now needed only for the reinforcing rods.

The first indication in Britain of an architectural idiom derived directly from the nature of concrete was seen in a number of smallish road bridges in Scotland designed by the engineer Sir Owen Williams, notably at Duntocher, Strathclyde (see page 186), built in 1925, at Tomatin, Highland, built in 1926 in collaboration with the architect Maxwell Ayrton (died 1960), and at Banavie, Highland, where in 1928 Williams replaced a nineteenth-century suspension bridge over the Lochy with a roadway supported on cylindrical concrete piers, leaving the original arched stone pylons in their place. These early reinforced concrete bridges were relatively bulky, possessing little of the muscularity and elegance of the concrete bridges the Swiss engineer Robert Maillart (1872–1940) was building in his country in roughly the same years, which set aesthetic standards that have never been surpassed, or of some impressively graceful concrete bridges in Sweden and America. Nevertheless Williams's Scottish bridges, Duntocher especially, showed more understanding than was previously evident in Britain of the forms logically to be derived from a process of pouring a fluid material into moulds.

This made it all the more disappointing that when Sir Owen Williams, already well known as a specialist in concrete, was entrusted in 1958 with a far more ambitious project than a series of minor Scottish road bridges – namely the design of all the bridges along the first of the new British motorways, the M1 from London to Birmingham, for which he had been consulting engineer since the motorway programme was conceived in 1945 – the bridges were far heavier and clumsier than the use of reinforced concrete demanded. This may have been partly due to Williams's attempt to reduce costs by standardizing as many of the structural components as possible, with the result that small bridges are supported by the same substantial pillars as those of the largest dimensions. It was also due to Williams's reluctance to employ the then newly developed technique of prestressing the reinforcement embedded in the concrete, a technique which roughly coincided with the motorway programme and to which is owed much of the lightness and elegance of the best modern bridges.

Prestressing, developed by another French engineer Eugène Freyssinet (1879–1962), involves putting the steel reinforcing rods (or more usually wires in the case of prestressed concrete) under tension before the concrete has set. Alternatively they can be placed in ducts within the already set concrete. Nunn's Bridge, Fishtoft, Lincolnshire, a small river bridge built in 1947, can probably claim to be the first prestressed bridge in Britain with the concrete poured *in situ* – the commonest method – although in the previous year a railway viaduct at Wigan had used precast concrete elements with prestressed reinforcement.

Nunn's Bridge in any case is of historic rather than aesthetic interest. The first bridge to set the style, and indicate the architectural potentialities, of the modern prestressed concrete bridge was built as part of the pedestrian circulation system of the South Bank Exhibition of the 1951 Festival of Britain, leading from the Waterloo entrance to the Festival Hall terrace. It was designed by Sir Ove Arup and had four spans, one at right-angles to the other three, cantilevered out from a central row of columns, and a deck less than two feet thick in the centre and only three inches thick at its tapered edges. Three of the spans survive, though with a building beneath them which appears to, but does not, support them. The fourth span has been replaced by a steel footbridge.

The first really substantial prestressed concrete bridge was built in 1952, at Northam, Hampshire, over the Itchen, and thereafter the use of this technique quickly became more expert and ambitious. Britain's programme of motorway building in particular owed a great deal to prestressed concrete, and in due course to further developments of it such as those employing precast and prefabricated components. It was first used for motorway bridges on the Preston Bypass in 1958 and with its help the design of bridges and overpasses was progressively refined. Some of the more recent motorway bridges, especially those on the M2 (London–Dover), the M3 (London–Southampton), the M6 (Coventry–Carlisle) and – perhaps most consistently of all – the M11 (London–Cambridge) are as shapely and elegant as any overseas. Most have been designed by the surveyors for the time being of the counties through which the motorways pass, by engineers attached to their staffs or by engineering consultants, sometimes with the advice of an architect appointed by the Ministry of Transport to oversee design standards along the whole motorway.

The individual motorway bridge is of relatively long span, sometimes with a central support between the two carriageways but often springing clear across the whole motorway so as to avoid obstructing the vision of fast-moving traffic. Its dimensions vary greatly, from the gigantic scale of the mile-long urban overpass such as that which leads the M4 out of London over the roofs of the western suburbs and the complex patterns of slip roads at the interchange point between one motorway and another, to narrow slender arches at pedestrian crossing-points. Problems other than structural that designers have had to solve include the treatment of the concrete surface, since it is a material that lacks intrinsic aesthetic appeal, and the treatment of the sloping embankments – motorways run for long distances at a lower level than the surrounding countryside – where they pass underneath a bridge. These problems have been fairly satisfactorily solved by a number of means: the surface quality with the help of textures provided by the type of shuttering into which the concrete is poured or by bush-hammering – roughening the surface after the concrete has set – or by contriving other textured finishes that will not break or stain; the sloping surfaces beneath the bridge, where grass will not grow, most frequently by facing them with pebbles or paving stones.

There is one other far-reaching development. Today the motorway and its bridges have to be looked at as a totality, and this has completed the process of isolating the road system from the geology of the landscape through which it passes, a process which began when engineers such as McAdam (see Chapter 2) devised smoother and more lasting methods of laying down road surfaces, so that by the early part of this century the ribbon of tar-macadam gave an unchanging character to the course of all main roads. Even within the memory of the present writer minor roads still derived their colours and textures from their locality; the pinkish soil of Devonshire gave its country roads a totally different look from, say, the grey-coloured grit that provided the road-making material of the north.

Relatively softer road surfaces suited horse traffic. Its almost total replacement by motor traffic led to a standardized black tar-macadam or a grey concrete becoming the surface material of all roads except the smallest country lanes. The even greater change brought about by the motorways is that in them cross-country roads are no longer a ribbon, rough or smooth, winding its way past unrelated objects such as houses, trees and bridges. Bridges on motorways have almost lost their separate identity. The total enterprise – roadways and slip roads, the white markings on them, their hard shoulders and revetted embankments together with their rapid succession of bridges – have become merged into one indivisible artefact laid upon the surface of the land.

A Selection of Bridges of the Last Hundred Years, listed by Counties (by Regions in Scotland)

(others listed under Railway Bridges, Suspension Bridges and Footbridges)

ENGLAND

Cambridgeshire

Wansford New Bridge over the Nene (a short way downstream from the medieval Wansford Old Bridge – see page 8). 1930. By Sir E. Owen Williams (consulting architect Maxwell Ayrton). Reinforced concrete. Three spans, two of 50 feet and the centre one of 110 feet. Smaller arches in the spandrels and between the double triangular cutwaters.

Cheshire

Widnes–Runcorn over the Mersey   1956, replacing the transporter bridge of 1901. By Mott, Hay and Anderson. Steel. Single arch of 1,080-foot span; when first built the largest steel arch in Europe and the third largest in the world.

Cleveland

Middlesbrough   Transporter bridge over the Tees. 1911, superseding a ferry-boat service. The largest of its kind in the world. By George C. Imbault of the Cleveland Bridge and Engineering Co. Steel truss of 565-foot span on lattice steel piers. 850 feet long (470-foot span between the towers) and 225 feet

Middlesbrough, Cleveland. Transporter bridge over the Tees. 1911. By George C. Imbault.

Borrowbeck Viaduct, near Tebay, Cumbria, on the M6 motorway. 1968. By Scott, Wilson and Kirkpatrick.

high. 160-foot clearance for ships at high water. Vehicles cross the river on a platform suspended by cables. It can also take up to 600 pedestrians.

Middlesbrough Newport lift bridge over the Tees. 1934. By Mott, Hay and Anderson. Steel arched girder which can be lifted horizontally to give 120-foot clearance above high water (clearance 21-foot when lowered). Span 260 feet. Steel towers 182 feet high supported on cast-iron cylinders.

Cumbria

Borrowbeck Viaduct on the M6 motorway just south of Tebay 1968. Engineers, Scott, Wilson and Kirkpatrick. Reinforced concrete. Three spans, centre one 160 feet, supported on sixteen circular columns. Deck of twelve precast post-tensioned beams. Parapets of contrasting white concrete.

Blackfriars Bridge, London: one of the red granite columns. 1865. By Joseph Cubitt.

Devonshire

Seaton over the estuary of the Axe   1885. By Philip Brannon. An oddity, being constructed of concrete blocks but having the form and architectural detail of a three-arch stone bridge. Perhaps the earliest surviving concrete bridge in Britain.

Kent

Cuxton carrying the A228 over the M2 motorway to Rochester   1962. By Freeman, Fox and Partners. Typical of a number of reinforced concrete overbridges on this motorway. Three spans with the piers integral with the deck and a rounded junction between. Iron railings.

Medway Bridge, part of the M2 motorway near Rochester   1963. By Freeman, Fox and Partners. Reinforced concrete. Three main spans over the Medway, the central one, of 500 feet, being the longest in Britain. Approach viaducts of eleven and seven spans. Total length 3,272 feet. Main road deck of prestressed concrete box-girders cantilevered from the main piers, the 100-foot gap between them being bridged by a suspended span of composite beam and slab construction.

London

Blackfriars Bridge over the Thames 1865, replacing Robert Mylne's bridge – see page 33; widened 1909 to make room for tramlines which made it, at 100 feet, the widest river bridge in Britain. By Joseph Cubitt (1811–72), chief engineer of the London, Chatham and Dover Railway whose own bridge runs close beside it. Five iron arches. Brick piers faced with Cornish granite and flanked by short Gothic-style columns of polished Ross-of-Mull red granite. Some very fine decorative ironwork which has however recently been obscured, and the lines of the bridge confused, by its sides being painted by the Greater London Council in a variety of ill-chosen colours.

Hammersmith Flyover linking central London to the M4 motorway 1961. By the G.L.C. architects and engineers (G. Maunsell, consulting engineers). Reinforced concrete. Road deck of precast units prestressed together to form one continuous structure. Sixteen spans. Total length 2,043 feet.

Holborn Viaduct over Farringdon Street at the point where Holborn Bridge, a medieval bridge said to have been rebuilt by Wren, once crossed the Fleet River 1863 (opened by Queen Victoria on the same day in 1869 on which she opened Blackfriars Bridge). By William Haywood (1821-94). Viaduct, concealed at both ends by buildings, 1,400 feet long and 80 feet wide. Central bridge over roadway in iron, 107-foot span supported on two rows of six hexagonal granite columns. The end columns continue upwards through the ornamental iron parapets to form pedestals for bronze statues representing on the south side Commerce and Agriculture and on the north side Science and Fine Art.

Tower Bridge over the Thames Bascule bridge in which the two halves of the roadway between the towers are hinged and can be raised to let ships through to the Pool of London below London Bridge, but are seldom raised now as large ships dock further down river (for the development of the design see pages 169–70). 1885-94. By Sir Horace Jones, architect, and Sir John Wolfe Barry, engineer. Towers of steel framing faced with Cornish granite and Portland stone on a brick backing; their bases of brick faced with granite. Approach roadways supported by chains passing over the towers and meeting within the iron lattice footway which spans between the towers 142 feet above high-tide level and is reached by hydraulic lifts. In spite of its relative fragility this footway had anti-aircraft artillery mounted on it during the First World War. It was closed to the public in 1909 but reopened in 1982. Main opening for ships 200 feet wide. Each bascule carried on four steel girders. The hydraulic mechanism for raising the bascules (each of which weighs more than

Hammersmith flyover, leading out of London to the M4 motorway. 1961. By the G.L.C.

1,000 tons) is housed within the towers and is powered by steam engines under the approach road. Since 1982 the mechanism has been open to visitors. The towers and abutments are elaborately Gothicized, the former being crowned with pinnacles and pointed roofs more French or Flemish in derivation than English. This architectural styling may be partly Barry's work because Jones died in 1887, only a year after building started. Its effect has been rather spoilt in recent years by the ironwork being brightly painted in several colours.

Waterloo Bridge over the Thames   1937–44, replacing Rennie's masterpiece – his handsome stone bridge of 1811. By Rendel, Palmer and Tritton, engineers; Sir Giles Scott (1880–1960), consulting architect. Reinforced concrete faced with Portland stone. Five very flat segmental arches each of 240-foot span including the land arches crossing the Embankment roadway on the north side and a pedestrian promenade on the south. They are not in fact true arches; four of the five are continuous beams with an arch-shaped lower profile and the centre span consists of two cantilever arms with a suspended span between.

Northumberland

Berwick-on-Tweed   Royal Tweed Bridge, within sight of the Old Bridge of 1610 (see page 48) and of the Royal Border Bridge (page 129); built to relieve the former which could not accommodate the weight of traffic. 1925. By L.G. Mouchel and Partners. Reinforced concrete. Four flat four-rib segmental

Waterloo Bridge, London. Over the Thames. 1937–44. By Rendel, Palmer and Tritton, and Sir Giles Scott.

Royal Tweed Bridge, Berwick-on-Tweed. 1925. By L.G. Mouchel and Partners.

arches springing from only just above water level with vertical posts filling the spandrels. The arches increase in span from 167 feet to 361 feet to allow for the difference in height between the two banks of the Tweed. The 361-foot span, when it was built, was the largest reinforced concrete arch in Britain.

Suffolk

Ipswich Orwell Bridge carrying the Ipswich Bypass over the main navigation channel of the Orwell downstream from Ipswich port and container terminal. 1980. By Sir William Halcrow and Partners. Prestressed concrete. Eighteen spans. The centre span, of 623 feet, is the longest prestressed concrete span in Britain. It is 135 feet high to allow ships to pass beneath. It is of cast-*in-situ* cantilever construction with a slightly curved soffit and single rectangular piers. The approach viaducts have 194-foot spans. Their twin rectangular concrete piers support separate box-girders, one beneath each carriageway. Total length 4,220 feet.

Holborn Viaduct over Farringdon Street, London. 1863. By William Haywood. See p. 179.

Tower Bridge, London. Over the Thames. 1885. By Sir Horace Jones and Sir John Wolfe Barry. See p. 179.

Orwell Bridge, Suffolk. On the Ipswich Bypass. 1980. By Sir William Halcrow and Partners. See p. 182.

Wearmouth Bridge, Sunderland, Tyne and Wear. 1929. By Mott, Hay and Anderson. See p. 183.

Sussex, East

Winchelsea Strand Bridge over the Brede. 1928, replacing a timber toll-bridge of 1810. By the engineers of the Ministry of Transport. One reinforced concrete beam of 30-foot span with its lower surface slightly curved. Mass concrete abutments. Bridge, parapets and abutments faced with Kentish rag-stone.

Tyne and Wear

Newcastle-upon-Tyne Swing bridge over the Tyne. 1876, replacing a stone-arched bridge of 1772 by Robert Mylne which impeded shipping and which had itself replaced a thirteenth-century stone bridge erected on the piers of a Roman bridge. By John F. Ure (1820-83). Pivoted on a central pier (an extension from one of the piers of the High Level railway bridge – see page 121) to give two openings for shipping each 110 feet wide. Arched steel girder 281 feet long. Two ribbed arches of the medieval bridge survive beneath it.

Sunderland Wearmouth Bridge over the Wear, $1\frac{1}{2}$ miles from its mouth. 1929, replacing a cast-iron bridge of 1793. By Mott, Hay and Anderson. Two parabolic steel arches of 375-foot span, 55 feet apart, from which the roadway is hung a little way above the springing. Stone abutments.

Yorkshire, South

Wentbridge on the A1 (Great North Road) over the Went valley south of Pontefract 1960. By S.M. Lovell, West Riding County Surveyor. Prestressed concrete – when it was built the largest of this type in Europe. Three spans between pairs of raking struts. Centre span 190 feet; side spans 140 feet. Road-deck, 100 feet above valley floor, one continuous cellular concrete beam.

Yorkshire, West

Lofthouse Intersection of the M1 and M62 motorways south of Leeds: a three-level circular interchange. 1966. By S.M. Lovell. Reinforced concrete. 800-foot diameter roundabout carried on four bridges over the two motorways to which it is connected by eight slip roads. Roundabout bridges supported on curved prestressed concrete piers with inclined precast concrete props of cruciform section.

Lofthouse interchange, West Yorks., at the intersection of the M1 and M62 motorways. 1966. By S. M. Lovell.

WALES

Glamorgan

Nant Hir Bridge over the river of that name, carrying the 'Heads of the Valleys' road, a new road built in 1962 to replace part of the old A465 between Hirwaun and Abergavenny   Typical of several high reinforced concrete bridges over valleys along this route. Engineers, Rendel, Palmer and Tritton; consulting architect, Alex Gordon (born 1917). Reinforced concrete. Single span of 184 feet, each arch consisting of twin ribs 13 feet wide; the road-deck, curved in plan, supported on the spandrel walls.

Gwent

Abergavenny over the Usk   1962. By Rendel, Palmer and Tritton; consulting architect, T. Alwyn Lloyd. Prestressed concrete; stayed girder construction. V-shaped supports between main river span. Short side spans.

184

Nant Hir Bridge, Glamorgan, on the 'Heads of the Valleys' road. 1962. By Rendel, Palmer and Tritton, and Alex Gordon.

Usk River bridge, Abergavenny, Gwent. 1962. By Rendel, Palmer and Tritton, and T. Alwyn Lloyd.

SCOTLAND

Highland

Grantown-on-Spey New Spey Bridge over the river of that name a mile south-east of the town and half a mile from the Old Spey Bridge built by General Wade in 1754 and now closed to traffic. 1930. By Blyth and Blyth. Reinforced concrete with bush-hammered surface. One low 240-foot segmental arch with dummy keystone. Two small round land arches.

Strathclyde

Clydebank over the Duntocher Burn 1935. By Sir E. Owen Williams. Reinforced concrete. One 80-foot span of parallel arches. Open spandrels beneath the roadway.

Concrete road bridge over the Duntocher Burn, Strathclyde. 1935. By Sir E. Owen Williams.

Queen's Bridge, Perth. Over the Tay. 1960. By F. A. Macdonald and Partners.

Glasgow   Glasgow Bridge over the Clyde, also known as Broomielaw Bridge and as Jamaica Bridge (recalling the one-time importance of the city's West Indian trade). 1894. Engineers, Blyth and Westland. Stone. Seven arches with three transverse arches within each pier. Eighty feet wide and thus, together with the Victoria Bridge also over the Clyde, second in width only to Blackfriars Bridge, London (see page 179). The first bridge on this site was built in 1767, was widened by Telford in 1821 and then replaced by him in 1833. Part of the granite facing of the present bridge came from its predecessor.

Tayside

Perth   Queen's Bridge over the Tay. 1960, replacing the Victoria Bridge, a steel-beam bridge of 1903 with cast-iron decorations. Engineers, F. A. Macdonald and Partners. Prestressed concrete. Three spans of 85 feet, 187 feet and 114 feet. The shallow curve of the underside of the deck gives a greater depth over one pier than over the other, compensating for a steep gradient necessitated by the two banks of the river being of different height.

187

10

Bridges Never Built

This chapter is of the nature of a postscript. As the Introduction explains, the bridges listed at the end of each preceding chapter of this book are limited to those still standing although in the main text a few bridges built but since demolished are referred to when they are of some significance in the history of bridge design or construction. This last chapter is concerned with a small number of bridge projects of outstanding interest which for one reason or another never reached fruition. They deserve a place in the history of British bridges either because they represent ideas ahead of their time or because they illustrate the imagination – sometimes the eccentricity – that the notion of a bridge has occasionally inspired in engineers and architects, including some of the most distinguished. They also reflect the different approach to the architectural opportunities offered by the challenge of a bridge as these were seen by men of various epochs. Most of those in the list that follows are for bridges over the Thames in London where leading architects were naturally eager to demonstrate their ability as bridge builders, but the Avon Gorge near Bristol was another location that inspired a great number of designs, including some that were little more than fantasies. One of those included here, Robert Adam's artificial ruin at Bowood, represents the idea, characteristic of the Picturesque movement, of a bridge as an ornament in a man-made landscape. Still others, such as Dance's twin stone bridges designed to replace the old London Bridge, introduce the conception of a bridge as an element in the layout of a Classical city. But the unbuilt bridge design that most assuredly represents ideas ahead of its day, also intended as a replacement of the old London Bridge, is one put forward by Telford in 1799. It was an iron bridge spanning the whole width of the Thames by means of a single arch. Few besides Telford had experimented at that time with iron as a structural material, and none in so bold a manner. His design, though defying all precedent, only just fell short of being built.

The project had its starting-point when James Douglas, a young mechanical

Bowood Park, Wilts. Stone bridge in the form of an artificial ruin. 1768. By Robert Adam.

engineer from Eskdale, Dumfries and Galloway (which was also Telford's birthplace), who had worked in America and recently returned to England, obtained an introduction to Telford in 1797. Telford was impressed by his talents and helped him to promote a number of inventions – which in the end came to nothing – that he had been working on, including a shearing machine and a 'Ball for destroying the Rigging of Ships'. In 1799 these two enterprising engineers began discussing in detail a project that Telford already had in mind for the replacement of London Bridge, the future of which had been a matter for dispute among politicians, engineers and the public for the past hundred years. As the nursery rhyme dating from that period reminds us, it was falling down, and in any case the rapid growth of the port of London in the eighteenth century required ships to be able to sail past it, to berths further up the river.

In April 1800 a standing Parliamentary Committee on the Port of London, set up by William Pitt after discussion by the City authorities had continued for four years without any action being decided upon, invited ideas for a new bridge at this point. Among the requirements were, in Telford's own words (quoted from a letter to his friend Andrew Little): 'to take down London Bridge, rebuild it of such dimensions as to admit ships of 200 Tons to pass under it – and form a new Pool for Ships of those dimensions between London and Blackfriars Bridges with a sett of regular Wharfs on each side of the River – This is with the view of saving Lighterage and Plunderage and of bringing the great Mass of Commerce near to the heart of the City.'

Later that year, in July 1800, Telford and Douglas breakfasted with the Parliamentary Committee and went on to view the site. Three days afterwards,

189

London. Project for a cast-iron bridge over the Thames to replace Old London Bridge. By Thomas Telford. 1800.

at a special meeting of the Committee attended also by Pitt, a resolution was passed in favour of 'rebuilding the bridge, the bridge itself to be of iron, on the improved plan of the Sunderland Bridge' (see page 81), 'with inclined planes added, parallel to the sides of the river, according to the plan suggested by Douglas and Telford; and the approaches, openings and masonry to be executed by Dance'. This was George Dance the younger (1741–1825) who was

then the City Corporation's clerk of works and who had already, in 1796, produced his own scheme for replacing London Bridge by two parallel stone bridges with a drawbridge in each – see the list at the end of this chapter.

It was a remarkable tribute to Telford's growing reputation that a Parliamentary Committee should accept without question his belief that an iron bridge of such dimensions was practicable. There was no precedent to go on;

the Sunderland bridge the Committee mentioned in its resolution had a span of 236 feet – then thought a great achievement. Telford proposed 600 feet for London Bridge. It is true that the Committee considered at the same time a five-arch iron bridge, an alternative design by Telford and Douglas, but Telford was confident that his bold single-arch design would be accepted, especially after it had been calculated that the revenue from the new wharves and warehouses would probably repay the cost of building it. A Commission of experts, of which John Rennie was a member, was appointed to examine it and Telford wrote in January 1801 to Matthew Davidson, one of his chief assistants, 'the Plan and Model have been universally admired, only the unprecedented Extent startles people at first, tho' most admit of the reasons in its favour, and all wish to have it done if practicable and advisable.'

There were some misgivings about the gradient. The bridge was to be high enough to give shipping a clearance of sixty-five feet and the ramped approaches (the 'inclined planes' proposed by the Parliamentary Committee) might, many thought, prove somewhat steep for horse-drawn vehicles, but the reasons why Telford's London Bridge was never built were more political than technical – the disturbed state of Europe discouraged the launching of any ambitious civil project. 'The French', Telford wrote, again to Matthew David-son, 'are driving all before them – The Austrians seem beaten at all points, and certainly must conclude a separate peace. How far we shall partake of the blessings or woes of the impending negotiations is beyond the Reach of my telescope – I am afraid they do not argue favourably to my projects, and to tell you the truth I shall not be surprised if the whole scheme is abandoned until some accident happens at London Bridge.'

And so it was. By the beginning of 1802 Douglas had disappeared to France and Telford had turned his attention to his many other interests. A new London Bridge, to a far more conventional design, was eventually begun in 1823 and completed in 1831, to be removed piecemeal to Arizona and replaced by the present one in 1967. As an answer to the problem of bridging a wide river Telford's single-arch design in iron is equalled in nobility only by a few medieval bridges such as those at Barnstaple, Durham, Hereford and Aberdeen, by the confidently Classical bridges of such men as Sir Robert Taylor, James Paine and Robert Mylne – to which should be added John Rennie's much lamented Waterloo Bridge – and by a few suspension bridges. Telford's project makes the design of Tower Bridge, for all the drama the latter extracts from its adaptability to new requirements, appear fussy and ill-digested. If the Romans had used iron they, one supposes, would have treated it as Telford did, and he revealed in the process the qualities that make him in many ways the most heroic figure in this book.

A Selection of Bridges Never Built, listed by Counties

ENGLAND

Avon

Clifton, Bristol, over the Avon Gorge   By William Bridges, an architect of whom little is known – not even the dates of his birth and death. The drawing in the R.I.B.A. Collection depicting his extraordinary project is dated March 1793. It is entitled 'Proposal for raising a Subscription to build a Bridge over the River Avon at the Rocks of St. Vincent from Sion Row Clifton to Leigh Down near Bristol Hotwell'. The great central arch was to be 220 feet high and 180 feet wide. The walls on either side of it, pierced by tiers of smaller

Clifton, Avon. Project for a masonry bridge over the Avon Gorge by William Bridges. 1793.

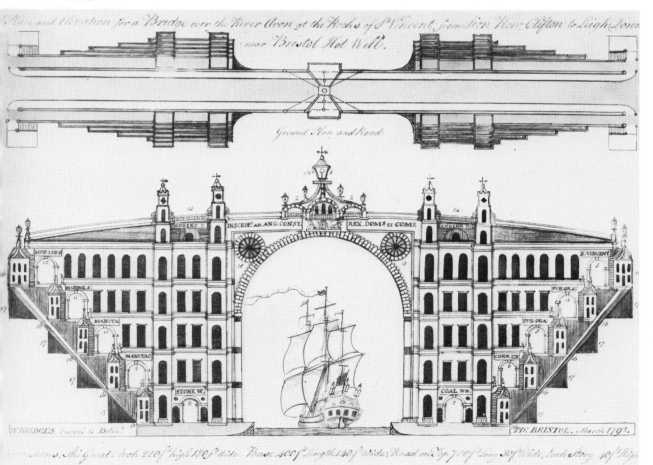

arches, were to be divided into storeys 40 feet high and to be thick enough to contain, among other things, a chapel, public offices and a corn exchange. The road along the top was to be 50 feet wide and 700 feet long. In the R.I.B.A.'s drawing an inscription along the top of the arch reads 'Ang: Const. Rex: Doms et Coms'.

Clifton over the Avon Gorge   1829. By Telford. This design for a suspension bridge was made after a competition held in 1828 in which Sir Samuel Brown, Isambard Kingdom Brunel and William Chadwell Mylne (1781–1863), son of the eighteenth-century bridge designer Robert Mylne, were among those who submitted entries. Telford was the judge but found no design suitable and so put forward one of his own. His bridge has two substantial Gothic towers rising from the river banks, crowned by pinnacles. It was liked by the public but not enough money was subscribed to finance it. His drawing is in the possession of the Institution of Civil Engineers. A second competition was held in 1830 in which Telford himself entered but the winner was Brunel – see page 143.

Clifton, Avon. Design for a Gothic suspension bridge over the Avon Gorge. By Thomas Telford. 1829.

GEORGE BENNIE RAILPLANE
CROSSING RIBBLE RIVER

Hesketh Bank near Lytham, Lancs. Project for a 'rail-plane' bridge over the Ribble. By George Bennie. 1928.

Lancashire

Hesketh Bank over the Ribble to a point near Lytham 1928. By George Bennie, a Glasgow engineer. Steel. Lattice-girders supported on lattice piers. Wide navigation span of trussed steel cantilevers. Part of a 'rail-plane' transport system invented by Bennie and designed to link Blackpool and Southport. Carriages were to be suspended from an overhead rail and propulsion was to be by means of propellers which, when put into reverse, would act as brakes. The bridge was to have a roadway threaded through the girders at a lower level. A 426-foot length of track, with a full-size carriage, was built for demonstration purposes at Milngavie, near Glasgow, in 1929 and Blackpool Corporation gave its approval to the project, but it was abandoned when tests of the electrical powering system resulted in total failure. Water-colour by Cyril Farey in the R.I.B.A. Drawings Collection.

London

Blackfriars Bridge Competition design by Sir William Chambers. Sixty-nine architects entered for this competition, held in 1759. It was won by Robert Mylne. Stone. Three semi-circular arches with rusticated voussoirs. Piers

embellished with statues framed by columns and pediments. Over the centre arch a tall screen of Corinthian columns terminating in niched pedestals crowned by sculpture. Drawing in the R.I.B.A. Collection.

London Bridge   Two parallel bridges to replace the medieval London Bridge. 1800. By George Dance the younger. Stone. Each bridge was to have six elliptical arches plus a smaller round arch in the centre, flanked by towers and supporting a drawbridge through which ships could pass. Between the bridge-heads on the north bank Dance planned a semi-circular piazza with the existing Monument (to the Great Fire of London) at its centre and a corresponding

left, *London. Competition design for a bridge over the Thames at Blackfriars. By Sir William Chambers. 1759;* below, *London. Project for two parallel bridges over the Thames to replace Old London Bridge. By George Dance. 1800.*

piazza on the south bank with a new monument in the form of an obelisk commemorating the recent naval victories. Aquatint by William Daniell belonging to the City Corporation.

London Bridge 1800. By Telford. Cast iron. One arch of 600-foot span. 65-foot clearance at high water. Arch built up of separate pierced cast-iron blocks. Ramped approaches on stone viaducts parallel with the river bank. Engraving by William Lowry after a drawing by Thomas Malton in the possession of the Institution of Civil Engineers.

Tower Bridge First proposal for a bascule bridge. 1878. By Sir Horace Jones. Superseded by the built design (for which Jones was architect and Sir John Wolfe Barry engineer – see pages 169 and 179), chiefly because the bascules could not be fully opened. Stone towers in a rather Germanic Gothic style with pointed roofs. Two iron arches with bracing between. Iron girder approach roads and bascules, the latter raised by means of chains. Pen and wash drawing in the R.I.B.A. Collection.

Westminster Bridge By Sir James Thornhill (1675–1734), who appeared in 1721 before a House of Commons Committee that was considering the

London. One of the discarded proposals for Tower Bridge: a bascule bridge by Sir Horace Jones. 1878.

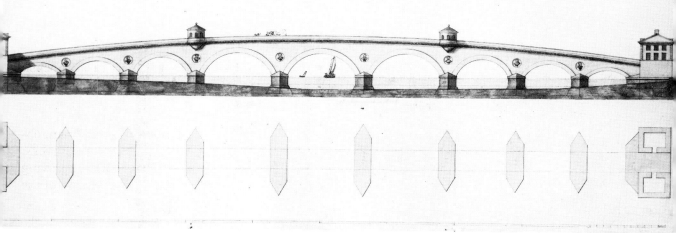

London. Project for Westminster Bridge over the Thames. By Sir James Thornhill. 1721.

possibility of a bridge over the Thames at Westminster. He declared the project to be practicable and his drawing, in the R.I.B.A. Collection, shows a bridge of nine segmental arches with triangular capped cutwaters on each pier. The balustrade over the third and sixth piers carries a circular turret and each spandrel has a roundel containing a sculptured head. A two-storey house stands at either end of the bridge.

Tyne and Wear

Newcastle-upon-Tyne Two-level road bridge. 1826. By Robert Stevenson, illustrated in the biography by his son David, published in Edinburgh in 1878. A project for linking the higher parts of the city on opposite banks of the Tyne by building a second bridge on top of the then existing one. Stone piers ornamented with twin pilasters supported on the piers of the old bridge. Cast-iron roadway. A two-level bridge was later constructed at the same point by Robert Stephenson (see page 121) but with the upper level a railway bridge and the road bridge hung from it.

Wiltshire

Bowood Park 1768. By Robert Adam, following the fashion for picturesque ruins, in this case 'in imitation of the Aqueducts of the Ancients'. Stone. Three semi-circular arches; balustraded parapet surmounted by equestrian sculpture. Adam's patron at Bowood (where the house was subsequently added to by C.R. Cockerell, altered by Sir Charles Barry and largely demolished in 1956) was the Marquess of Lansdowne. Drawing in the possession of the Soane Museum, London.

Glossary

abutment
: The structure supporting a bridge at either end and resisting its horizontal thrust.

arch
: A curved structure spanning an opening. It can take various shapes: semi-circular; segmental (part of a circle); elliptical (part – usually half – of an ellipse); pointed (two curves meeting at the crown) etc.

arch-rings
: Rings or slight recesses round the outer edge of an arch.

cantilever
: Projecting beam or other structure supported at one end only.

cast iron
: Iron shaped by being poured molten into moulds.

catenary
: The curve taken up naturally when a chain, cable etc. is suspended from either end.

centering
: The temporary wooden framework used in the construction of an arch which holds it up until it is self-supporting.

concrete
: A mixture of pebbles etc., sand, cement and water poured into moulds and hardening into a stone-like substance. *Reinforced concrete* has steel rods inserted where the tensile stress is greatest to give extra strength. *Prestressed concrete* has its reinforcement (wires instead of rods) put under stress before the concrete has set. In *post-stressed* (or post-tensioned) *beams* the stressing is done afterwards.

corbel
: To project from the face of a wall; a stone that does so.

Glossary

crown	The uppermost point of an arch.
cutwater	Projection beyond the base of the pier of a bridge, rising above water level, to protect it; strictly, a projection shaped to divide the flow of a stream but the term is often used for any such projection – see *starling*.
dentils	Small square projections enriching the under side of a cornice.
dressed stone	Stonework given a smooth surface by working with tools.
haunch	The curve of an arch between its springing and its crown.
humped arch	An arch of a bridge with a shape that gives it a steep rise and fall.
keystone	The uppermost stone (or brick) in a stone or brick arch which holds the voussoirs in place.
laminated wood	Layers of wood glued or pinned together to make strong arches or beams.
obelisk	A square ornamental pillar tapering towards the top and ending in a pyramid.
pediment	A triangular feature or moulding in Classical architecture over a niche or opening.
pier	The supporting structure between two or more arches or girders of a bridge.
pylon	A tower, used in the present context for the towers between which the chains or cables of a suspension bridge are slung.
refuge	A recess formed in the parapet of a bridge, usually by building out over a pier or cutwater, to enable pedestrians to shelter from traffic.
rib	A ridge of stonework projecting from the soffit of a bridge to strengthen it.
rustication	Masonry with recessed or otherwise prominent joints.

Glossary

shuttering	The framework, usually of wood but sometimes of steel, into which liquid concrete is poured and which is removed when the concrete has set.
soffit	The under side of an arch, beam etc.
span	The distance between the supports of an arch or beam.
spandrel	The triangular space between the springing and the crown of an arch.
springing	The point at which an arch begins to curve upwards from its supports.
starling	A protective structure at the foot of a pier, of which a *cutwater* (which see) is one form.
steel	An alloy of iron containing carbon and possessing greater strength and hardness.
string-course	A moulding running horizontally along the face of a wall.
stringer	The sloping part of the structure of a staircase on which the ends of the treads are supported.
truss	A number of lengths of timber, iron or steel framed together so as to bridge a space economically.
turnpike	A road on which tolls are levied to repay the cost of building it or meet the cost of maintaining it.
vermiculated	Stonework decorated on the surface with a worm-like pattern.
voussoirs	The tapering stones or bricks out of which an arch is built up.
wing-walls	The side walls of the approach to a bridge, continuing the line of the parapet.
wrought iron	Iron made in bars by hammering when softened by heat; stronger in tension and less brittle than cast iron.

Bibliography

Barbey, M.F., *Civil Engineering Heritage: Northern England*, Thomas Telford, 1981 (published on behalf of the Institution of Civil Engineers; further volumes covering other regions proposed)

Chappell, M., *British Engineers*, William Collins, 1942

Colvin, Howard, *Biographical Dictionary of English Architects: 1600–1840*, John Murray, 1978

de Maré, Eric, *The Bridges of Britain*, Batsford, 1954
The Canals of England, Architectural Press, 1950

Gibb, Alexander, *The Story of Telford*, Alexander Maclehose, 1935

Hopkins, H.J., *A Span of Bridges*, David and Charles, 1970

Jervoise, Edwyn, *The Ancient Bridges of the South of England*, 1930
The Ancient Bridges of the North of England, 1931
The Ancient Bridges of Mid- and Eastern England, 1932
(published on behalf of the Society for the Protection of Ancient Buildings)

Johnson, S.M. and Scott-Giles, C.W. (joint Editors on behalf of the Public Works, Roads and Transport Congress, London, 1933), *British Bridges: an Illustrated Technical and Historical Record*, 1933

Marshall, J., *Biographical Dictionary of Railway Engineers*, David and Charles, 1978

Pevsner, Nikolaus (and collaborators), *The Buildings of England* (by counties from 1951 onwards), Penguin

Phillips, Geoffrey, *Thames Crossings*, David and Charles, 1981

Rolt, L.T.C., *George and Robert Stephenson*, Longman, 1960
Isambard Kingdom Brunel, Longman, 1957
Thomas Telford, Longman, 1958

Bibliography

Ruddock, Ted, *Arch Bridges and Their Builders: 1735–1835*, Cambridge University Press, 1979

Scott-Giles, C.W., *The Road Goes On*, Epworth Press, 1946

Sealey, Antony, *Bridges and Aqueducts*, Hugh Evelyn, 1976

Smiles, Samuel, *Lives of the Engineers*, John Murray, 1861–2

Walters, David, *British Railway Bridges*, Ian Allan, 1963

Acknowledgments

The author's thanks are due to the following for their prompt and helpful replies to letters seeking facts and figures: the archivist of the Institution of Civil Engineers, various regional officers of the National Trust (especially in connection with Chapter 3), the librarian of the National Railway Museum at York and the Director of Civil Engineering at British Rail (Chapter 6), the Cement and Concrete Association (Chapter 9), the R.I.B.A. Drawings Collection (Chapter 10), the British Architectural Library, the county archivists of Buckinghamshire, Cumbria, Devonshire, Lancashire and Oxfordshire, the Derbyshire county librarian and the principal librarian of Newbury, Berkshire.

Thanks for help and advice are also due to Mr Michael Robbins, F.S.A., Mr John Piper, C.H., Mr Eric de Maré, Mr M.F. Barbey and Mr John Donnelly.

The author and publishers are grateful to the following for permission to reproduce black and white photographs: the Ancient Art and Architecture Collection (Ronald Sheridan's Photo-Library), pp. 118, 120; the *Architectural Review*, p. 156; B.T. Batsford Limited, p. 10; Christoph Bon, p. 31; Ben Boswell, p. 24; Cement and Concrete Association, pp. 163, 167, 177, 180, 184, 185 above and below, 187; Eric de Maré, frontispiece, pp. 7, 11 above and below, 14, 17, 19, 22, 23 below, 25, 27, 29, 35, 40, 42, 43, 49, 56, 57, 59, 66, 69, 71, 72, 80, 86, 88, 91, 96, 97, 98, 99, 101, 103, 110, 119, 124, 126, 128, 130 above and below, 134, 143, 146, 148, 149, 150, 155, 159, 162, 181; Edinburgh City Libraries, p. 58; Guildhall Library, pp. 196–7 below; the Institution of Civil Engineers, pp. 190–1, 194; A.F. Kersting, pp. 12, 13, 15, 46, 53, 65, 73, 74, 127, 144, 151; Douglas McGhee, p. 152; Edward Piper, pp. 18, 133, 176; Derek Pratt, pp. 23 above, 93, 100, 104, 106; J.M. Richards, pp. 116, 135, 136, 137, 145, 178; Royal Commission on Ancient Monuments (Scotland), p. 77; Royal Commission on Historical Monuments (England), pp. 32, 41, 158; Royal Institute of British Architects, pp. 193, 195, 196 above, 198, 199; the Sefton Photo-Library, p. 161; Brian and Sally Shuel, pp. 9, 47, 48, 54, 68, 83, 95, 102, 160, 164, 182; the Trustees of Sir John Soane's Museum, p. 189; Strathclyde Regional Council, p. 186; Derek Widdicombe, p. 132.

Acknowledgments

Colour plates are reproduced by kind permission of: Ace Photo Agency/Ed Baxter, opposite p. 87 below; the Ancient Art and Architecture Collection (Ronald Sheridan's Photo-Library), opposite p. 39 above, opposite p. 102 above, opposite p. 134 below, opposite p. 183 below; British Tourist Authority, opposite p. 23 above; Cement and Concrete Association, opposite p. 183 above; A.F. Kersting, opposite p. 22 above, opposite p. 38 above, opposite p. 39 below, opposite p. 151 above; the National Trust, opposite p. 86 above and below; Susan Okell, opposite p. 22 below; John Pasmore, opposite p. 167 below; Derek Pratt, opposite p. 102 below, opposite p. 103 below; J.M. Richards, opposite p. 38 below, opposite p. 150 below, opposite p. 166 above; Brian and Sally Shuel, opposite p. 87 above, opposite p. 103 above, opposite p. 150 above, opposite p. 151 below, opposite p. 166 below, opposite p. 167 above, opposite p. 182 above and below; Derek Widdicombe, opposite p. 134 above, opposite p. 135 above and below; George Young Photographers, opposite p. 23 below.

Index

Where possible, individual bridges are listed under the town or city in which they are situated; where the bridges are in the countryside they are listed under their own names or localities. Numbers in italics indicate illustrations.

208